Suburban Dictionary

The Subtle, the Funny, and the Snarky

A Slang and Sarcasm User's Guide

Timothy Fay

Dedicated to those who survived,
and to those who did not survive,
the housing crisis and
Great Recession of 2007 to 2013.
God bless us all.

If you have a garden and a library, you
have everything you need.

Marcus Cicero, Rome, First Century BC

Invitation

This book is a user's guide to suburbanese, as well as a guide to the quirky behavior found in the burbs. The snarky and the cheeky make many appearances, along with generous helpings of sarcasm. Euphemisms, a hallmark of suburbanese, get "special" treatment. We give a nod to cul-de-sac personalities, such as the neighborhood eccentric and the Goth kids. Even the recluse a few doors down makes a (rare) appearance.

There was a need for a book about that talks about things that can get you into trouble—sex and drugs are examples—but that does so with expressions that won't get you into trouble should you care to repeat them.

Words from overseas make the cut if they are amusing or if they strike a chord about family life. For instance, "Nappy Valley," a Brit phrase for a neighborhood that is overrun with toddlers, squeaked by. "Wet leaves," a phrase that Japanese wives use for unemployed husbands, was also included. (Unemployed husbands stay at home all day and can't easily be swept away, like wet leaves.)

Most of all, amusing terms about family and life in the burbs were admitted. "Niblings," a catchall term for nieces or nephews, is an example. "Lollipop lady," the British term for a crossing guard, is another. "Solar panel," a term for a bald spot on the back of a bloke's head, was also included. A few fun but familiar words make appearances. Such entries include noogie, wedgie, and flat tire—ever-popular teen pranks.

I gathered these expressions from years of reading (nearly anything) and listening to podcasts, TV, co-workers, and family. Working as a newspaper reporter and serving in the Army Reserve also helped. In most cases if a word has an entry in this book, it's being used by the public. A few exceptions are words that were coined in *Suburban Dictionary* and noted as such. One example is "Tes-hole": a Tesla driver that is quite impressed with himself or herself.

In just a moment, we'll check out the words and expressions in *Suburban Dictionary*. But first, I should warn you that collecting slang, zingers, and bolts of sarcasm is quite addictive.

Please enjoy *Suburban Dictionary* and please visit our website www.suburbanese.com[1]

---

1. http://www.suburbanese.com

Suburban Dictionary Timothy Fay
Numbers

18: The key number when giving gifts at a bar mitzvah or bat mitzvah. Cash gifts should be in multiples of eighteen, such as $36, $54, or perhaps $180.

201(k): Result of frequent withdrawals from someone's 401(k) retirement plan.

420: Term for pot smoking. Also a designated time (4:20 p.m.) when some smoke weed. The cannabis equivalent of **beer thirty** or happy hour. Also signifies the date of April 20th, which some proclaim as "national cannabis day." April 20th is nearly considered a holiday in some parts of California.

B-9: The parking space number (or room number) you should opt for at a hospital, especially if you're getting a "suspicious lump" checked out.

R2D2: Nickname for a short, round person. Named for the resourceful droid of *Star Wars* fame. Filmmakers say the name sprang from "reel 2, dialog track 2," later shortened to R2D2.

Symbols

#: Hashtag. Also called an octothorpe. Known as a pound sign in telephone lingo. A hashtag with a word or phrase, without spaces, highlights a (supposedly) trendy topic. ***Example***: *#girlscoutcookies.*

...: Ellipsis. These three dots, midsentence or midtext, mean that part of the message must be left to the imagination. ***Example***: *She went over to his place. They talked ... She took the bus home the next morning.*

- A -

abandominium: A vacant or abandoned property. Also refers to a building taken over by squatters.

abandoned swimming pool: For neighborhood skateboarders, an instant skate park. Just remove water.

ABC: 1. American-born Chinese. A person of Chinese blood who grows up with a strong knowledge of American culture and little or no "accent" when speaking English. **See also: *Banana, Chinglish, Chiwi.*** **2.** "Apply Butt in Chair." Cajoling expression for anyone tackling a big project. **3.** "Always Be Closing." Slogan of salesmen/saleswomen.

abstinence: A useful word in the suburbs, which means avoiding sexual activity or other mischief. Reasons for abstinence range from religious or well-being considerations to simply being unlucky. **See also: *dry spell*; *lackanookie.***

actually: Term that can denote surprise that someone succeeded. ***Example:*** *"I've learned not to tell my mother-in-law that her cooking **actually** tasted good."*

Adolf Hitler: Golf slang for having to take two shots in the bunker (sand trap).

adorkable: Dorky yet adorable.

A F: As f**k. ***Example:*** *"These cronuts are good A F."*

See also: *cronut.*

a few fries short of a happy meal: Cuckoo; stupid.

afraid of the dark: Golf term for a ball that stops just short of the hole and refuses to drop in.

aging hipsters: Term preferred by some over "old folks," or "senior citizens."

AirGarage: Company modeled after Airbnb, but for renting parking spaces rather than homes. Homeowners near college campuses and other venues earn cash from customers wanting to ditch their cars temporarily.

Air-conditioning the whole neighborhood: Traditional scolding given by moms and dads to a kid who leaves the door open. Often heard as "Are you trying to air-condition the whole neighborhood?" In reality, when you run a heat pump in the winter, you *are* trying to air-condition the whole neighborhood. **See also:** *mansplanation.*

Example: Mom yelling at son: "Are you trying to air condition the whole neighborhood?"

Teenage son: "Yeah, Mom. I thought it was time to give back to the neighborhood."

Alaska: The largest state in the US. Alaska does indeed have suburbs. Just ask the residents of the **Anchorage** suburb of **Wasilla,** who elected Sarah Palin as mayor. Palin would go on to become governor of Alaska. She also was nominated for US vice president in the 2008 election.

alcohol: An intoxicating hydrocarbon compound commonly found in the burbs. You can hardly say the word suburban without saying "bourbon." The word "alcohol" is of Arabic origin, and it means "the essence."

al desko: Eating at your desk; a play on the word "alfresco."

algos: Algorithms. Formulas based on customer behavior that websites use to maximize company profits.

Example: Co-worker # 1: "I just tried outsmarting a travel website, and I found nothing but shitty prices."

Co-worker # 2: "Can't fool the algos."

All juice, no seeds: Motto of men who've had a vasectomy.

"All adults must be accompanied by children.": Humorous inversion of the usual warning: one theater chain notes that at children's movies, adults must be accompanied by children.

aloof: Detached from those around you. An indispensable word in the suburbs. *Example: The dad in the original 1964* Mary Poppins *movie is sometimes described as uptight, but is probably better described as aloof.* **See also:** *avoidance.*

"Alrighty then!": Expression used to denote awkward surprise or embarrassment. **See also:** *AWK.*

Amish-ish: A person who observes some, but not all, aspects of Amish life. Can also apply to events, such as an "Amish-ish" wedding, in which both Amish and "English" (the Amish word for non-Amish folks) mingle awkwardly.

Anaheim, California: Los Angeles suburb, home of the "Mouse House," Disneyland. **See also:** *Disneyverse; Orange Curtain.*

"And how!": Expression meaning "And then some!" *Example: Nine-year old son: "Dad, did you play football in high school?"*

*Dad: "**And how!**"*

"And I get that.": Expression used to (attempt to) elevate someone's opinion to fact. *Example: "If (blank) is elected, he will save the country. And I get that!"*

ankle bracelet: Euphemism for an ankle monitor, a tracking device worn by those under house arrest or worn by other detainees. Not exactly a fashion accessory. *Example:*

Actor Paul Rudd's character in the 2018 film Ant-Man and the Wasp *sported an ankle bracelet.*

antiromantic comedy: Comedy that involves romance but doesn't have a happy ending.

aracial: Someone who is "raceless" and seems to avoid getting pigeonholed into any particular racial group.

"Are you planning on getting out of the business?": Snarky response sometimes given when a business owner (such as a restaurant owner) asks you to post a review on Yelp or similar websites.

Armenians: One of the first so-called ethnic groups to venture into the suburbs. Armenians in **Southern California** have been noted for their success in business as well as for their baklava (a pastry often made of paper-thin dough, nuts, and honey). *Example: Do yourself a favor and never say around an Armenian that baklava is a "Greek" dish.*

ASMR: Autonomous Sensory Meridian Response. A mouthful describing any event, especially an auditory experience, that triggers a tingle on your spine or commands heightened attention. YouTube has countless "ASMR" videos. A common example: an ear massage video, in which the masseuse also whispers into the mic.

assclown, ass clown: A stupid jerk; a clueless person. A term often used in the ever-popular 1999 movie *Office Space.*

Astroturfing: The often-deceptive practice of giving an organization or a message the appearance of having grassroots, Joe Blow support.

Large corporations sometimes try this when trying to pass, or block, a referendum proposal. **See also: *reeferendum.***

attractive nuisance: Legal term describing a real estate feature, such as a swimming pool, that is a potential hazard yet lures children and others. **See also: *hot mess.***

au pair: A nanny or domestic servant from overseas, usually a female in her late teens to late twenties. Au pairs use the arrangement as a chance to travel and are considered *au pair* (on par in French) or equal to the host family.

auntrepreneur: An aunt or any older woman who is talented in business affairs.

avoidance: Popular suburban method for "dealing" with conflict: by simply evading it (or attempting to do so).

avuncular: Someone who seems like uncle material, in appearance or behavior. **See also: *Dutch uncle.***

Awful House: Snooty nickname for Waffle House chain of diner restaurants, popular in the southeastern US. Some claim you can judge the severity of hurricanes – and virus scares – by noting whether Waffle House locations (usually stalwarts) are closed.

AWK: Shortened version of "awkward", often used when responding to accidentally shared text messages. **See also: *Alrighty then.***

- B -

"Baby up in this bitch": The 2020s replacement for "Baby on board" stickers on SUVs and mini-vans. *Welcome to the '20s.*

"baby sister": **1.** A younger sister. **2.** Charming, "slightly-off" interpretation, by recent English speakers of the term "baby sitter."

back end: Term used in business settings to help steer the conversation away from detailed explanations. ***Example:*** *"Sorry about the excessive fees. We'll take care of that on the back end."* **See also:** ***Don't worry about it.***

back into a mattress: To have sex; to prepare to have sex. A vintage term for a vintage activity.

backronym: An "acronym" explanation of a word origin that someone invents, long after a word was developed. For instance, word-historians say that one explanation for "posh," "port out, starboard home" was cleverly invented long after the word "posh" was common. Reportedly "posh" originated in 1800s England, referring to a nattily-dressed person.

Example: *SABENA, the nowdefunct Belgian airline, was sometimes the subject of a snooty backronym: Such A Bad Experience, Never Again.*

"Back up.": Expression meaning "Excuse me, but I strongly object to something you just said."

Example: *Guy at a bar: "I think* Game of Thrones *is sort of stupid."*

Woman at a bar: "Umm, back up!"

bae: Term of endearment used by teens and others. Some claim this is a shortening of "babe." Others say it's an initialism of "Before Anyone Else," as in "I loved you BAE," but that may be a **backronym.**

bag rat: Golf caddy.

bailiwick: An area of jurisdiction or authority.

Example: *"What was that* **Chicago** *cop doing in* **Milwaukee?** *That's not his bailiwick."*

baked in, baked into the cake: Real estate or business term meaning "already figured into the price, so don't get any smart ideas."

Example: Elaine: *"Let's buy that property across from the casino. Word is that the city is going to build a school there!"*

Jerry: "Yeah, but that's already baked into the cake."

Banana: Term used, usually jokingly or good naturedly, for an Asian-American who is yellow on the outside, but white (or perhaps simply "Americanized") on the inside. **See also:** *white rice.*

bank-owned: Euphemism for a property that has been repossessed from the borrower.

BAP: Black American princess. **See also:** *CAP.*

bark park: Term for dog parks, where dogs can "mingle" without leashes. Pet owners also meet and mingle in these venues.

bay window: **1.** A paunch or beer belly. **2.** A window that protrudes from a building facade. **See also:** *Nature trail.*

BC: **1.** Before Christ. **2.** Before computers. **3.** Before coffee.

Example: *Sorry I did such a bad parking job this morning. That was B.C.*

beast: A **gym rat** who has taken bodybuilding to extremes.

beer goggles: Term for a condition in which members of the opposite sex (or the same sex) become more appealing in proportion to the amount of beer that has been chugged.

beer thirty: Happy hour; or any other suitable beer-drinking opportunity. **See also:** *420.*

Be yourself, but not *too* much.: An adage that is useful in the workplace, especially for those prone to seek attention or to yammer on most of the day.

biflation: A situation in which consumers simultaneously face inflation for some needs and deflation for other items. This describes the US economy just after the Great Recession of 2008. Housing prices plummeted, while inflation took hold in goods such as gasoline, food, and gold. **See also:** *shrinkflation.*

Big Box Reuse: Absorbing book by Julia Christensen about reusing vacant retail stores. One amusing reuse: a former Kmart in **Austin, Minnesota**, that has been **repurposed** as the Spam Museum. (The kind of Spam found in a can.) **See also:** *repurpose; Spam.*

Big D, The: 1. Divorce. **2.** Dallas, Texas.

bike balls: 1. A variation on *truck nuts* for bicyclists. These taillights hang from the back of the bike seat and are visible to motorists. Bike balls are thought to be an amusing way of increasing visibility and safety. **2.** An unfortunate condition that affects MAMILs ("Middle-Aged Men In Lycra"). **See also:** *truck nuts.*

bicycle ninja: Cyclists who travel around after dark without lights or protective clothing, and pop out of "nowhere."

bike salmon: Urban cyclist who "swims upstream," going the wrong way on a one-way street.

billionaire next door: Phenomenon in which a billionaire chooses to live in a rather ordinary upper middle-income neighborhood, perhaps even next door. Berkshire Hathaway CEO Warren Buffett famously lived frugally for decades in a middle-class home in the burbs of **Omaha, Nebraska.**

birdbath: Real estate term for a paved area where water collects but is not meant to do so. **See also: *rooftop garden.***

Blaxican: A person of Black and Mexican descent.

blogger: An unemployed person. Sounds much hipper than the 1990s equivalent, ***consultant*. Example:** *If someone says he is a blogging consultant, he probably hasn't had a job for a very long time.*

blue flu: Term for an informal strike by police officers, in which many cops simultaneously stay home because of the "flu."

blue room: Construction worker slang for the Port-a-Jon or portable toilet, so named because of the blue plastic walls. Also called the ***green room,*** *bog* (UK), or *dunny* (Australia).

Example: *Question: "Haven't seen Phil for a while. Anybody seen him?"*

Answer: "He's in the blue room."

See also: *throning.*

Blue tool: An annoying person (a tool) who uses his or her Bluetooth device to have a cell-phone conversation near you.

BMW: 1. Big Mormon Wagon. Slang term for SUVs and minivans used by Mormons to transport (sometimes) large families.

2. Bayerische Motoren Werke or Bavarian Motor Works. Popular up-scale German-designed vehicles. Jokingly said to mean *Bitch, Moan, and Whine,* referring to the all-too-often whiny Yuppies who drive BMWs.

Bob Ross: Ultra-relaxing host of the *Joy of Painting* TV show. Part painting lesson and part mind massage, this show has aired on PBS for decades. Has a cult following with grandmas, stoners, and just about everybody in between. **See also: *ASMR; happy accidents.***

boink: To have sex, which does occasionally occur in the suburbs. Also called *bonk, shag,* (UK), and *root* (Australian).

bonkers: Crazy.

boo birds: Sport fans who frequently boo their sports teams.

boomerang kids: Grown children who move "back" to their parents' home. Also refers to someone who returns to their hometown after living in a big city. ***Example:*** *Smaller inland cities in California, such as Fresno, seem to have attracted **boomerang kids** in recent years.* **See also: *crowded nest.***

boss's boss: Term heard more than occasionally in business. For instance, some say those who want to climb the corporate ladder should dress like their "boss's boss." (Might be a bit awkward for a man whose boss's boss is a woman.)

Example:

Disgruntled customer: "I want to talk to your boss's boss."

*Call center employee: "Actually, **I am** my boss's boss."*

bot: 1. Robot or robot-related. Examples include a "cambot" (robotic camera), or "fembot," a robot designed to look or act womanly.

2. Old-school Wall Street shorthand for "bought."

Example: Bot 100 shares @ 44 and ½.

Botox: Marketing term for *botulinum toxin*, a neurotoxic protein (yikes!) used in cosmetic touch-ups in suburban "med spas."

See also: *Vampire facial.*

bourbon: A corn-mash based whiskey, very popular in the burbs (and elsewhere). Traditionally made in Kentucky.

Example: It's hard to say suburban living without saying "bourbon."

See also: *Whiskey Belt.*

BRB: Be right back. Used in both speech and texting. (This meaning has superseded "Big Red Button," a device that will trigger a detonation of some sort.)

breastaurant: A restaurant that features female waitstaff in revealing attire. The term appears to have developed in the early 1990s, 'round the same time as Hooters restaurant chain in the US.

bris: Jewish ceremony of circumcision.

Bris Vegas: Ha-ha name for **Brisbane, Australia,** and its many casinos.

BritBox: Streaming TV service with myriad British shows and movies. Has a growing following in U.S. households.

broken fan belt: Reason given by many when asked why they settled in cities such as **Tucson, Arizona,** or **Albuquerque, New Mexico,** while supposedly en route to California.

bronies: Grown men and women who are fans of the *My Little Pony* TV show, which was otherwise the realm of little girls.

Brooklyn Park, Minnesota: A suburb of **Minneapolis, Minnesota**. Former professional wrestler Jesse *"The Body"* Ventura served as mayor of Brooklyn Park from 1991 to 1995. A few years later, he was elected governor of Minnesota, in an upset by Ventura.

bro science: Word-of-mouth tips concerning dieting and fitness exchanged between "bros". Often has little scientific proof, leading to the bro science abbreviation of "B.S." **See also:** *gym rat.*

brotein: Protein-packed snacks, such as "brotein bars" or jerky, often consumed by body builders and other gym rats. **See also:** *gym rat, reverse diet.*

brown flu: A work slowdown or informal strike by UPS (United Parcel Service) workers.

BTW: By the way.

Buc-ee's: A **Texas** phenomenon. Buc-ee's is a chain of massive filling stations (and gift shops). Prides itself on ultraclean restrooms. Buc-ee's claims there's two reasons to stop there: number 1 and number 2. (Ha ha). The chain recently expanded into **Alabama,** skipping over **Louisiana** and **Mississippi.**

Buckhead: Upscale suburb with an often mispronounced name, in north **Atlanta, Georgia.** Buckhead now rivals downtown Atlanta as a center of commerce.

Bud Light haze: Viewpoint of many suburban dads, especially on holiday weekends, who perceive their surroundings through a Bud Light haze.

budtender: A server of pot at marijuana dispensaries, especially at a "recreational" dispensary.

bum wheel: A bad leg.

buppies: Black upwardly mobile professionals. **See also:** *chuppies.*

burbclave: Blend of "suburb" and "enclave." An extension of today's gated communities. The term was featured in *Snow Crash,* a 1992 novel by Neal Stephenson. In this novel, which was "futuristic" at the time, suburbs exist as entirely gated enclaves with their own governments and police forces.

Burbs, The: Entertaining Tom Hanks movie of the 1980s. Strange goings-on next door ignite interest among the neighbors. After a one-week staycation, the main character decides to go on a *real* vacation. **See also:** *staycation.*

business casual: Dress code in the workplace that does not require men to wear ties or women to wear hose in most cases. Business casual is yet another oxymoron in workplace lingo, along with **office park**, "positive attrition," work "flow", and ethical hacker.

butt hut: Outdoor smoking area, often under a tarp or canopy.

buttinski: (noun) Someone who often "butts in" or interferes.

buuut ...: Elongated form of "but", used when reluctantly admitting to an embarrassing deed, or reluctantly disagreeing with someone. *Example: "I'm not saying these cargo pants make it easy to sneak snacks into the movie theater, **buuut ....***"

buyer's remorse: Discomfort with a recent major purchase decision, especially with real estate buys. Psychologists say this is partly because a done deal reduces the buyer's options from an array of possible choices to a single slice of reality: the purchased home, with its flaws now on display. The good news is that most buyers eventually move on emotionally and view their new house as "home".

- C -

Cabin Porn: Mesmerizing website and book from 2015 by Zach Klein and Steven Leckart displaying beckoning cabins in both wilderness and in-town areas. A refreshing alternative to **McMansions**. **See also: *Dog Cabin.***

Cablinasian: Term by golf pro Tiger Woods for a person who is a blend of Caucasian, Black, American Indian, and Asian descent.

Cadillac Desert: Landmark 1986 book by Marc Reisner telling how the arid American West was remade into a near Garden of Eden. Thanks to dams and canals, vast areas were primed for farming ... and later for sprawling suburbs.

Example: 1960s-era housing developer # 1: "I'm going to put in a huge housing tract on the edge of Palm Springs."

Developer # 2: "You can't build there. It's desert!"

*Developer # 1: "When I'm done with it, it's gonna be a **Cadillac Desert**."*

California carpool: When a group of family members or co-workers drive to the same location in separate cars.

campanology: Term used at Trader Joe's grocery stores for their low-tech bell-ringing "Morse code" system. One bell means to open a register. Two bells means there are questions at a register. Three bells means a manager is needed. Three long bells, two short bells, one long bell means... just kidding.

Can I get that in writing?: Conversation tactic in which a threat is converted into a promise.

Example: Boyfriend: *"If you don't get rid of that stupid dog, I'm moving out!"*

Girlfriend: *"Can I get that in writing?"*

Can I help you?: Euphemistic way of saying "What are you doing here?" or (if said in a harsher tone) "You're not supposed to be here."

Can you work on that?: Suburbanese expression meaning "Would you *please* get your shit together?"

candy van: Mostly humorous term referring to a van that a sex offender might use to lure children. However, teens usually use this term to refer to a beat-up, old family minivan that could use an upgrade.

cannabiz: Term for pot and pot-related businesses that some claim are in the midst of a **Green Rush**.

canned air: Spray cans, also known as gas dusters or compressed air. Used for "cleaning" keyboards or other surfaces that can't (or won't) be cleaned by hand.

Example: She found that spraying canned air was very handy to avoid hearing her boss's bullshit "updates."

canon: 1. Term used by fans of a fiction writer to denote the original author's "official" book content, as opposed to subsequent reviews or fan-written sequels. **2.** Term used to distinguish scriptures from subsequent commentary. ***Example:*** *Teens will sometimes say that a fan-written sequel to the* Harry Potter *series is "not canon."*

canoodle: 1. To "neck" or to make love. **2.** To cajole or persuade. One theory on canoodle's origin springs from earlier times when chaperones were a constant concern (or constant irritant) for teenagers. Canoe rides in suburban parks and elsewhere offered an escape from chaperones and therefore allowed for necking, and possibly more.

CAP: Chinese American princess.

Captain Hook: Baseball slang for a manager who will take a pitcher out of a game, often at the first inkling of trouble. Also applies in the non-sports world to a manager who fires an employee.

carbecue: A car fire.

Carbuncle Cup: British architecture award given annually for the ugliest building completed in the UK during the year. Named for carbuncles, which are unsightly boils or sores.

cat café: A café, often in larger cities, in which cats are available for playing with or for watching, as part of "kitty therapy." Also refers to a cat adoption or rescue center.

cat lady, crazy cat lady: A lady in the neighborhood—usually middle-aged or older—who has or attracts many, sometimes dozens, of cats to her property. Maybe the cat lady should visit a cat café, instead of *owning* so many cats. **See also: *Grey Gardens.***

cat's-eyes: Reflectors embedded in the pavement of roads to denote lane dividers.

CBD: Term for cannabis and related chemicals. CBD refers to cannabidiol, a chemical extracted from pot. Some say that CBD has helpful medical uses, with less side effects than sister chemical THC. The term CBD has also become a marketing term used by pot "dispensaries". A "CBD" sign is *probably* more discreet than a "WEED SHOP" sign. **See also: *MMJ.***

CEDM: Christian electronic dance music. A Christianized (and usually blander) version of **EDM.**

chain (transactions): British term for the chain of transactions in many real estate deals. If buyer A is not able to sell her home, she won't be able to purchase a home from seller B, who in turn will not be able to purchase his sought-after home from seller C, thus "breaking the chain". **See also:** *musical chairs.*

changing of the guard: Metaphor for a change in leadership or "the end of an era." An example is grown children taking over responsibilities from their elderly parents. Often has a bittersweet connotation.

Chardonnay: Light white wine that is a favorite of moms, housewives, and others in the burbs. A refrain sometimes heard is, "Chardonnay all day!"

charm of days gone by: Term that can mean either: **1.** Something exuding charm from earlier times or, **2.** Something that had charm in days gone by, but is no longer charming.

checked all the boxes: Someone or something that meets the basic requirements for a position or role, but is lacking in pizzazz or sex appeal.

cheeky: Sassy or irreverent in an amusing way.

cheese and rice: Substitute for the expression *Jesus Christ!* Best used in a drawn-out pronunciation.

Chelsea: 1. Famous upscale suburb of **London, England. 2.** Neighborhood on the west side of **Manhattan**. A major Chelsea attraction is the High Line, an appealing city park built on an abandoned elevated railroad track.

Chelsea tractor: British term for an oversized four-wheel drive **SUV** that is used by aging **Sloane Rangers** for shopping trips and for hauling children around, but not for off-road driving. **See also:** *BMW, Sloane Rangers*

cherry on top: An act or comment that lifts already rude behavior to cad levels, originating from the phrase "the cherry on top of the turd".

Example: *When that bitchy customer dropped an f-bomb, that was the cherry on top!*

chick lit: Friendly name for books written (mostly) for women and girls. ***See also: lad lit.***

chicken butt: Rather common children's response when asked, "You know what?"

Example: *Dad: "You know what?"*

Ten-year-old daughter: "Chicken butt!"

Chicken legs: Skinny legs, when attached to someone with broad shoulders.

Chicken Wire: Amusing name for the email newsletter of restaurant chain Chick-fil-A.

Chinglish: A blend of Chinese and English spoken by Chinese American teenagers and others. **2.** English-language signs in China featuring laugh-inducing awkward translations. (Somewhere at this moment a Chinese person is probably writing about awkward translations of Chinese by English speakers.) **See also: *Chuppie, Singlish.***

Chipot-lane: Drive-through lane that Chipotle grill is adding at many locations.

Chiwi: A Kiwi (New Zealander) with Chinese ancestry.

chronic: Adjective (or noun) used to describe rather potent cannabis.

Example: *Phil learned that his sixty-something neighbor, who suffers from back pain, smokes pot every morning (about 10 a.m.). Chronic weed for chronic pain.*

Chuppie: A Chinese or Chinese American yuppie. A Chinese young upwardly mobile professional.

Circle K: Convenience store chain that is popular in the western United States. The chain's logo appears to spell out "OK."

clickbait: Obnoxious or titillating web links or headlines designed to lure web users. Proof that the human race is not necessarily advancing. **See also:** *clocksucker.*

climax home: Largest or most expensive home a person will own in his or her lifetime. For many, their lifespan involves a starter home, a climax home, and in some cases a "downsized" home in senior years. In recent years, the term "die-in" home has sprung up: a home that the owners have determined will be their last.

clink, the: jail. Also known as the big house, hoosegow, con college, or the country club. In Britain, prisoners are said to be hosted "at Her Majesty's pleasure," since the Queen is technically their hostess.

clock sucker: Someone who wastes your time. **See also:** *time suck.*

Club Fed: Sarcastic name for minimum-security prisons that often house white-collar dipshits. **See also:** *skate.*

cocktail liberal, champagne liberal: A wealthy or upper-middle-class person who embraces the causes of liberals and/or the working class. Also called a limousine liberal. In the UK, a "champagne socialist."

comfortable: Old-school term which means well-off financially.

comp: To provide goods or services for free.

Example: "I had a lobster dinner last night. I told the waiter there was a fly in my soup and, well ... I got the whole meal comped."

comparisonitis: Anxiety or depression that can arise when someone makes a less than circumspect comparison of their accomplishments or possessions to those of others. Often aggravated by social media.

competitive landscaping: One-upmanship in the arena of yard landscaping, common in the burbs. Some choose to opt out of this, risking scorn from neighbors.

condomillennium: A condominium occupied mostly by millennials.

"Congratulations, you just won a trip to the principal's office.": Sarcastic refrain used by school teachers toward a disrespectful child. If we want our children to learn sarcasm, we must teach them at an early age.

consultant: Term used in the 1990s for an unemployed person. This word has now been surpassed by the term *blogger*. **See also:** *cotton broker.*

control "F" it: **1.** Search command used in e-documents. **2.** Workplace slang meaning "F" it.

Example: *Co-worker # 1: "You know what, I'm really getting sick of these spread sheets."*

Co-worker # 2: "You know what, it's Friday afternoon. Just **control 'F'** *it."*

cosplay: A Japanese term, now used in the US, meaning "costume play." Refers to devotees of a genre that wear costumes to celebrate an event or media phenomenon. Commonly seen on Halloween but also at events such as *Stars Wars* movie premiers, at ComicCon, and at Civil War re-enactments. **See also:** *period rush.*

Costcop: The attendant at the Costco exit who ensures that the contents in your cart match your receipt. A sort of reverse greeter. **See also:** *sample jam.*

cotton broker: A vintage Southern US euphemism for an unemployed person or a playboy.

cougars: 1. Fierce mountain lions that are occasionally seen in, or near, suburbs of the western United States. **2.** Fierce older women who seek out younger men.

county line: Frequent location for landfills and correctional facilities. Counties that appear rectangular in shape often build landfills in the county's corner. **See also:** *NIMBY, PIITBY, YIMBY.*

crazy-rich: Extremely wealthy. **Example:** *Some say there is a growing divide between the merely or "barely" rich and the crazy-rich. The crazy-rich often view the rich as lazy. And stupid.*

creative accounting: Also sometimes called "cooking the books." Thought to be one of the causes of the 2008 recession, as iffy loans were at that time deemed acceptable by some accounting firms. Chroniclers say the term creative accounting originated in the 1967 Mel Brooks movie, *The Producers.*

cronut: Deep-fried combination of a croissant and a donut.

Co-worker # 1: *"So, tell me one thing you really enjoyed on your trip to Louisville."*

Co-worker # 2: *"Kentucky-fried cronut."*

crooked numbers: Baseball slang for numbers other than one or zero. In a low-scoring game, a sportscaster might say, "We need some crooked numbers on the scoreboard." **See also:** *goose egg.*

crowded nest: A play on "empty nest." A house in which grown children have returned home. Also describes a home in which children above college age have never achieved "exit velocity". **See also:** *Failure to Launch.*

crunchy water: Ice.

crunk: Getting crazy and drunk, preferably at the same time.

Cuban: Golf term for a ball that stops just short of the hole, and needs one more revolution.

cul-de-sac: French term, more pleasant sounding than "dead-end street." In French, it means "bottom of the bag." The scheme is popular for homebuyers in the burbs, but is also a bit of a dead end for traffic flow in the neighborhood.

cute meet: Term used in romcoms and chick lit describing how the two main characters meet early in the story. Usually the two meet in some sort of clash, such as a fender-bender collision. Later in the story, the characters usually become lovers.

- D -

Daggy: Unfashionable or uncool, but usually in a charming way. A mostly British and Australian term. Australians enjoy "daggy jumper" day, a parallel to "ugly sweater" day in the U.S.

Dallasification: Term used by some in **Austin, Texas,** for growing "over-commercialization" of the city.

damn with faint praise, damning praise: To give a slight compliment to someone (or something) and thereby insult.

Example:

Man on a date: "So, how did you like the restaurant?"

Woman on a date: "Well, at least the ice was cold."

dawn patrol: Golf slang for those who wake up early and tee off at sunrise.

deadmalls.com: Interesting, somewhat mesmerizing website that tracks the fate of dead or dying shopping malls. Quite interesting are malls that closed only a few years after opening, or that went out of business before they *even opened* for business. **See also: *urban exploration.***

deferred maintenance: Euphemism for the condition of homes that need, or soon will need, quite a bit of work. Very common during the recession of 2007 to 2013. Let's hope there's not a "relapse" of this during the virus scare of year 2020.

Deluxbury: Nickname for Duxbury, an upscale Boston suburb in the South Shore area.

demonym: Word for the inhabitants of a particular place.

*Examples: People from **Glasgow, Scotland***: *Glaswegians.*

Las Vegas, Nevada: Las Vegans.

Liverpool, England: Liverpudlians.

Phoenix, Arizona: Phoenicians.

designated drunk: Anyone besides the designated driver in a group, or at a party. Can also mean the most annoying person in a group of revelers.

desert rat: 1. A person who lives in a desert area of the western US and often takes pride in rejecting a conventional lifestyle. As suburbs spread outward into the desert, some desert rats feel increasingly "fenced in." **2.** Friendly term for long-term residents of the Southwest US.

dessertarian: A sweet tooth: one who emphasizes desserts in their "diet."

Dick Hertz: Moniker often used at conventions and other gatherings when you're asked to fill out and wear a "Hello, my name is ..." sticker.

dimple: A hollow or false bottom on a bottle designed to skimp on contents, but maintain the appearance of the same bottle size. **See also:** *shrinkflation.*

din-din: Kids' (and parents') word for dinner. Also used by **cat ladies** to call their pets for mealtime.

disconnect: To take a break from electronic devices (as in a "digital detox").

Example: *Harry: "I'm going to walk the dog."*

Sally: "Aren't you bringing your cell phone?"

Harry: "No, that's my time to disconnect."

Sally: "Alright, then. Take a nice long walk."

See also: *FOMO, JOMO.*

Disnerd: A "grown up" who is ultra-enthused and savvy about Disney movies and theme parks.

Disneyverse: The Disney "universe" of entertainment. Ranges from Disney movies, TV, and music, to more recent acquisitions, such as Marvel Comics, and the *Star Wars* franchise and the "interesting" live action remakes of classic animations.

divorce: Legal cessation of a marriage. Divorce had an uptick during the recovery from the Great Recession, around the years 2013 and 2014, when warring husbands and wives decided that they could now *finally* afford their own places.

Example: *"If someone asks you what's the leading cause of divorce, that's easy: marriage."* **See also: *emancipation.***

divot: 1. A hairpiece or wig worn by a man to cover a bald spot or **"solar panel." 2.** Dislodged turf gouged out by a golf swing. **3.** Dislodged turf, in this case from the hooves of polo ponies. Polo match observers are expected to replace the divots during the halfway break at polo matches. **See also: *solar panel.***

doga (dog yoga): Partaking in yoga with pet dogs. Offered at some yoga locales as a de-stressing therapy.

dog cabin: A dog-house built in log-cabin style.

dogvorce: 1. A break-up with a dog. **2.** When an owner is forced by circumstance to give away a pet dog.

"Don't worry about it.": Expression that often means "not gonna happen." Can also mean "none of your business."

Example: Lackluster college student: "When is graduation?"

College professor: "Um, don't worry about it."

door dorks: Those who stand in the doorway of an office and talk at length without entering. Also refers to employees who talk loudly just outside a meeting room while waiting for the current room users to finish their meeting.

double-dip: 1. To rudely reinsert a potato chip (and your germs) into a dipping sauce after you've taken a bite. **2.** To twice take advantage of an organization's retirement programs. For instance, a retired Federal worker who has a pension *and* draws Social Security.

drain surgeon: Sarcastic term for well-paid plumbers, especially in expensive areas such as **Manhattan** or **San Francisco**.

drained swimming pool: An instant skate park for neighborhood skateboarders. Just remove water.

droll humor: An offbeat or odd sense of humor. Not necessarily a requirement but definitely a boon for those living in the often-humdrum burbs. The Brits are particularly noted for this brand of humor.

drybacks: US residents who have moved to Mexico. Especially refers to those who don't have proper documentation.

dry spell: A period of time in which no sex is had, either intentionally or unintentionally. Can also refer to a period without drugs, alcohol, or other "activities." **Example:** *"Ever since I bought my Prius, I seem to have had a dry spell for some reason."* **See also:** *abstinence.*

dual equipment: A person with ... dual equipment.

DUDE: Developer under delusions of entitlement. A land developer who feels entitled to special treatment and rapid project approval. Slang among city planners.

DUI-cycle: A moped or scooter used by someone who has lost his or her driver's license due to driving under the influence of alcohol (or other substances).

dumb ask: A stupid question or a person who wastes time by asking unneeded or uninteresting questions. **See also:** *clock sucker.*

DUMBO: Neighborhood in **Brooklyn, New York.** So named because it's Down Under (the) Manhattan Bridge Overpass. Locals claim the word "overpass" was added so that the neighborhood would not be simply **DUMB.**

dumpster fire: A situation that is both dangerous and messy. A fiasco to avoid.

Example: *"You don't want to get involved in that project: it's a dumpster fire, and you're gonna end up getting sprayed with burning trash."*

Dunks: New England term for Dunkin' Donuts, also simply called Dunkin'.

Dutch treat: A group event in which each member pays his or her own tab. **Example:** *I thought my aunt was going to pay for everyone's dinner last night, but it was a Dutch treat.*

Dutch uncle: An uncle or any older male figure who gives frank and unwelcome advice. It's thought that this term originated during the joint reign in **Britain** of William, a Dutch king, and Mary, a British queen. Some Brits reportedly tired of advice from William and his henchmen. Another theory contends that this term simply stems from the famously (or infamously?) outspoken nature of the Dutch. **See also:** *avuncular.*

DWB: Don't write back. Icy way of ending an email or text exchange. Not recommended for the workplace. **See also:** *NSFW.*

- E -

Easter egg: 1. An insider joke or bonus message that is hidden (but findable by geeks and others) in a movie, book, or video game. Mischievous employees sometimes work Easter eggs into otherwise stiff-collar business meetings. **See also:** *treasure hunt.*

E.B.A.: Everything but anchovies. A popular heaping of toppings on pizza.

EDM: Electronic dance music. Something resembling EDM was called techno in the 1990s.

egg beaters: Whirling rooftop ventilators, a common sight in many neighborhoods. **Example:** *Many have proposed using egg beaters as a power source, turning them into micro wind generators.*

eggetarian: A vegetarian who eats eggs but no other animal products. Also called an ovo-vegetarian.

elephant tracks: Handyman slang for the "tracks" or dents left on wood when hammering and missing the nail. A common sight in suburban households where repairs are done by DIY dads. Or at least that's what we've been told.

emancipation: A person or group being granted freedom. **2.** A teenager or other child who gains independence before the normal age of majority. In an episode of the ABC TV Show *Suburgatory*, teenage daughter Tessa pushes for emancipation. Cheeky!

entitled: Describes someone feels they are *owed* special treatment. Common in upscale suburbs, and widespread also in most other neighborhoods.

EOM: End of message. Often used in the subject line of emails, sometimes as the written equivalent of a mic drop.

Example: *I am breaking up with you. EOM.*

epic: Amazing, excellent. The new "awesome." Often used by teens and twenty-somethings. *Example: That cronut was epic!*

ethnoburb: Suburb in which a particular ethnic group congregates. An example is **Monterey Park (MP)**, north of downtown Los Angeles, which has a large Chinese and Vietnamese population. MP features an endless array of beckoning restaurants.

Everyman's rights: Scandinavian term referring to the right of "every man" or woman to wander on private land and gather items such as berries, nuts, and mushrooms, as long as private areas such as yards are respected and little or no damage is done to the land. This is considered a basic right of citizens in Sweden and Finland.

EVOO: Extra virgin olive oil; term used in restaurants to impress customers.

exitate: To hesitate, while finding your bearings, after exiting a building or an elevator. Sometimes used as a ploy to avoid walking alongside colleagues after work.

expresshole: Term used by comedian Rich Hall. Someone who abuses the express line at the supermarket, buying seventeen items instead of staying under the fifteen-item limit. **See also:** *Tes-hole.*

extreme value shopper: Retail euphemism for an extreme cheapskate.

- F -

Fabio: Nickname sometimes used by moms for male pet dogs with long hair.

facilities: Polite term for the restroom.

Failure to Launch: A comedy from 2006 starring Matthew McConaughey and Sarah Jessica Parker about a thirty-something son who lives with his parents. The son views living at home with his parents as quite acceptable, until his parents hatch a scheme. **See also: *boomerang kid*** and ***crowded nest.***

familystickers.com: The company to credit—or blame—for millions of stick figure decals on the back windows of SUVs. A typical "sticker" shows a family of five, plus a dog, standing in a line and facing you as you're stopped at a red light. Variations include a *Star Wars* family or a zombie family. *It's how suburban folks have fun.*

family office: Management office overseeing the assets of very wealthy families. Typically includes a lawyer, a financial planner, and an accountant at a minimum.

Fast Times at Ridgemont High: A crowd-pleasing film from the 1980s about life in suburban L.A. that especially highlights life in the mall.

favela: Brazilian-Portuguese word for a suburban "slum" of a major city, often on a steep hillside. Some hillside favelas in **Rio de Janeiro** have spectacular views of the city and its beaches. In recent decades, many favelas have seen improvements in housing and other services.

feature preacher: Business slang for a sales rep who touts the many features of a product rather than focusing on a client's key needs.

feck: One of the more recent substitute words for f**k, popularized by the British/Irish sitcom *Father Ted*.

feedback sandwich: Criticism that is "sandwiched" between two compliments. A slippery feedback technique that has received both scorn and praise, often in that order. If someone makes a slew of mistakes, this technique can result in a multilayered sandwich.

feng shui: The Asian parallel of geomancy, the orientation of buildings in order to incur good fortune. A sought-after quality when buying homes for some Asians. Also a consideration for "non-Asians" who realize they might eventually sell their homes to Asian-Americans, or Asian-Brits, and so on.

filing system: Someone's system of organizing ideas. Especially refers to someone who has difficulty absorbing new ideas. **Example:** *Nephew # 1: "Why is Uncle Jerry so upset about electric motorcycles?"*

Nephew # 2: "Doesn't fit into his filing system."

FILTH: Failed in London, Try Hong (Kong). Term used by some Hong Kong residents for Brits who move to Hong Kong to try their hand in business there.

fine: 1. A suburbanese term that often means someone's mood is quite rotten, but the person would rather not talk about it. **2.** Word used to pretend to agree with someone while actually disagreeing: especially infuriating when used in marital arguments.

Example: Peggy: "How was your day at work?"

Al: "Fine."

Finger Plan: City planning scheme in which fingers of development radiate out from the central business district, with green belts in between. Denmark's **Copenhagen** is a model for this.

firing range (indoor): An increasingly common feature in some upscale homes. Also found in suburban gun clubs in strip malls.

fixer-upper: 1. Marketing term for a home that needs quite a bit of repairs. As comedian Kevin Nealon notes, there's a fine line between a "fixer-upper" and a "tearer-downer." **2.** Also used since the movie *Frozen* to refer to a possible romantic partner with lots of potential.

Fixer Upper: Very popular "reality" TV show on HGTV starring Chip and Joanna Gaines and based in **Waco, Texas.** The show aired from 2013 to 2018.

flat tire: Kids' and teenagers' prank in which someone walking just behind you steps on the heel of your shoe, pulling your shoe partly off.

fleece: An expensive, hard to shed car lease.

flexetarian: A supposedly "vegetarian" who will occasionally eat meat. **See also:** *pescatarian.*

flipping, illegal: Also known as **phlipping.** Observers blame much of the housing downturn of 2008 to 2013 on illegal house phlipping. *Example: In a flip scam, buyer A buys a home for $200,000 in a hot market. He then asks a conspirator appraiser to make an inflated appraisal. Buyer B, also a conspirator, buys the home for $350,000 using borrowed funds. Buyer B has no intention of living in the home and walks away from the mortgage. Buyers A and B split the "fast-buck" profit.*

flipping, "legitimate": Buying a house with the sole intention of quickly selling the home at a profit. Many aim to sell the home shortly after performing a shoddy remodel.

folly: A building resembling a castle, but built after the age of castles.

FOMO: Fear of missing out on an experience or perhaps on a business venture. Some describe this as a fear of missing the latest news among friends, resulting in frequent "checking in" on e-devices, which can lead to **comparisonitis**. See also: *comparisonitis, JOMO.*

fongool (fangool): Americanized version of an Italian phrase meaning "f**k you!"

food coma, food-induced coma: Sleepiness after a heavy meal.

Example: After eating the "triple" burger from In-N-Out, Brooklyn went into a food coma.

foot wedge: Golf slang for illegally nudging the ball with your foot.

freecycle: To reuse something that has been (or would have been) discarded, thereby saving funds. A play on the word "recycle."

freegan: A play on the word "vegan" (total vegetarian); refers to those who take discarded food and other items from dumpsters or trash heaps. Some do this to go green; others to save money; and some simply for the fun of the "treasure hunt".

freemium: Pricing model in which a service is offered gratis at a basic level, with an upgrade available for a charge. YouTube operates in this way, with an ad-riddled service for free and an ad-free version available at a premium.

Free ninety-nine: Stolen, or "hot," referring to the "price" of shoplifted items. *Example:*

Teenager # 1: "How much did that pair of sunglasses cost?"

Teenager # 2: "Free ninety-nine."

free-range children: Term used by some for children growing up prior to, and during, the 1970s. Describes how kids roamed the neighborhood for many hours at a time, whereabouts unknown.

freeway professors: College instructors who combine part-time jobs at two or more colleges (to make ends meet), and thus spend much of their lives on the freeway.

"Friday light": Term used in radio traffic updates to proclaim a happy Friday commute with light traffic.

Friendsgiving: Gathering with friends, rather than family, at Thanksgiving. A staple on the popular 1990s sitcom *Friends*.

Friendsmas: Similar to **Friendsgiving**; Christmas spent with friends.

friend-zone: When a person has been shunned romantically but not otherwise, they have been relegated to the "friend zone." Can be a noun or a verb. Possibly a pun on American football's "end zone." ***Example: I finally asked her out, and she friend-zoned me.***

"Fries before guys": Girl-centric term that places loyalty among "besties" over dating and perhaps over guys generally.

Fri-yay: Friday. Also a greeting, as in "Happy Fri-yay!"

frunk: Blend of the words "front" and "trunk." A trunk in the front of a (usually) electric car, such as a Tesla. Triggers a bit of *deja vu* for those who remember 1970s-era Volkswagens.

Example: *Thirteen year-old brother: "Where in the Tesla do I put the suitcase?"*

Sixteen year-old brother: "In the trunk."

*Thirteen year-old: "I tried, but there's an **engine** in there."*

*Sixteen year-old: "In the **frunk**, dumbass!!"*

FUBAR: Classic term meaning fu**ed up beyond all recognition.

(The) **fun never stops:** Sarcastic expression used when meeting yet another roadblock.

Fun-Tier Capital of Texas: Awkward nickname for the city of **Austin, Texas.**

fur son: 1. Someone's male dog or cat: a "fur son." **2.** Any furry pet; a "fur person."

- G -

gaby, gayby: Baby of a gay couple.

gap decade: A *gap year* that has stretched a bit too long.

gap year: Purposely taking a year off from your professional career. So named because a gap appears on your resume between jobs or college stints. Also used to retroactively claim that an idle stint was always intended as a gap year. ***Example:*** *After working for those jerks, I needed a gap year. At **least** a year.* **See also:** *starter retirement.*

Garage Mahal: An ostentatious garage at a home, especially at a *McMansion.* Has room for four or more vehicles and may feature a tile floor. For some males, this is a **man cave** on steroids. **See also:** *man cave; sick.*

garden view: Marketing term used to describe a property that does *not* have a view of a beach or nearby body of water. In hotel settings, this usually means a parking lot view.

gazumped: British term for being outbid when making an offer on a home, even after your offer was informally accepted.

Gen Rx-er: Slang term for millennials who are dependent on pharmaceuticals.

Gen XXL: Term for overweight members of Generation Z (Gen Z; born mid-1990s to mid-2000s), named for the XXL symbol for *double extra-large* on clothing tags.

Give him/her the flick: To dump someone. **See also:** *serial monogamist.*

glamping: Camping without "roughing it." For instance, staying in rustic but well-furnished cabins or yurts.

glowy thing: Term for a key element in superhero movies. Non-fans of Marvel films say the plots are usually about finding a glowy thing and thereby saving the universe.

golden handcuffs: Attractive benefits designed to prevent an employee from leaving a job. Especially refers to deferred compensation.

goldfish: Someone with a short memory span.

golf clap: A gentle, quiet clap after a golfer scores. Also used in non-golf settings to show lukewarm enthusiasm.

"Good luck with that": Expression noting that that your idea has serious pitfalls, and you're therefore "on your own."

good times: Semi-sarcastic term for an episode that was "less than ideal."

goose egg: 1. A zero score in a sporting event. **2.** A swelling or bump on the head, called a hematoma by health-care givers. **See also:** *crooked numbers; rearrange your face.*

"gotcha question": A question in which the asker already knows the answer, and is setting up a "gotcha." Frequently used in marital arguments. **See also:** *I'm just curious.*

Goth: A style of music and dress prevalent among teens and twenty-somethings in the burbs of the 1980s and 1990s. Still has a following today. Marked by dark clothes, dyed black hair, and music by bands such as Bauhaus. Committed Goths often show contempt for "weekend Goths" who dress down for work.

"Grace": Sarcastic address for someone who has goofed or otherwise stumbled. *Example:*

Co-ed # 1: "Damn it, I dropped my drink."

Co-ed # 2: "Way to go, Grace."

grazing: Casually eating or sampling. Especially refers to grazing samples at venues such as Costco.

Green Room: Construction worker slang for a portable toilet or "porta-potty." Also known as a **Blue Room.**

Green Rush, the: A "rush" of operators into the legalized pot biz.

Grey Gardens: Absorbing 1975 documentary film about Edith Beale and her daughter Edie Beale, who lived in a dilapidated 1897 mansion in **East Hampton** on **Long Island** in **New York.** Growing increasingly reclusive, the Beales lived in the home for fifty years, amidst raccoons, cats, and overgrown weeds. **See also:** *recluse.*

grow a tail: To do number two.

guh-ross!: Teen expression of how gross something is, but one notch higher than the usual "Gross!" *Example:*

Teen # 1: "Can you help me pop this zit?"

Teen # 2: "Guh-ross!"

gym rat: A frequent gym visitor; especially those who socialize long after finishing their work out. Sometimes viewed as a "pain" by gym employees. One trend noted on the TV show *Extreme Cheapskates*: gym members who take a shower there when not working out, to save on their water bill.

- H -

haboob: Arabic word for dust storms. Thanks to TV weather spinners, this is now a household word in the Southwest US.

had for a song: Old-school term meaning bought at a very cheap price. **See also:** *Free ninety-nine.*

HAGS: Have a great summer. Often noted on high school yearbooks.

hair helmet: 1. Excessively primped hair with plenty of gel or other product. The hair is thus held tightly in place, even on windy days. Often designed to hide a **solar panel.**

2. Amusing bicycle helmets available from online retailers. Though made of tough plastic, the helmets are designed to look like "big hair" or Afro wigs. **See also:** *solar panel.*

halal (hallal): Permitted under Islamic law, especially regarding food preparation. A parallel to the Jewish concept of *kosher.* "Halal" signs are increasingly seen in some ethnoburbs around the US. One interesting twist is "Chinese Islamic" restaurants in parts of **L.A.** and elsewhere.

halfbacks: Retirees who move from the northeastern United States to **Florida** and then move "*half* (way) *back*" home. For example, retirees might move from **New Jersey** to **Florida** and discover that they dislike the expense and crowdedness of coastal Florida—not to mention the hurricanes. The retirees will then move roughly halfway back home, to somewhere like **North Carolina** or **Virginia.**

hall pass: Term for a situation when a spouse is permitted to see others. Situations involving hall passes rarely end well.

hangry: Blend of "hungry" and "angry." **See also:** *pingry.*

happy accidents: 1. Term used by famed and ultra-chill PBS TV artist Bob Ross for "mistakes" when painting: "There are no mistakes, only happy accidents." **2.** Term adopted by stoners to refer to any idiocy that ends up with a good outcome.

"has landed": Expression which means something momentous has just occurred.

Example: Little brother: "Who is that at the door?"

Big brother: "It's the delivery guy. The pizza has landed."

head snap: A sudden turn of the head, with a glaring look, to challenge someone.

herbal remedy: A euphemism for pot.

hick-hop: Term that loosely describes a mix of hip-hop or rap, and country music.

hideout: Kids' term for a concealed area where they can temporarily "hide" from parents or siblings. Can range from thick shrubbery to nearby woods, or a vacant lot.

high maintenance: Any person who needs constant attention or assistance.

hillbilly heroin: Oxycontin and other opioid medications. Some claim that abuse of these drugs increased dramatically during and after the Great Recession circa 2008 to 2013.

himbo: A male bimbo. A dimwitted, good-looking male. Also called a "mimbo" (man-bimbo).

hipster: A term that comes up now and then in the suburbs. A hipster is usually in their twenties or thirties, enjoys indie or alternative music (and lets you know about it), wears thrift shop clothing, and often embraces a vegan or green lifestyle. Though rare, hipsters can be found in the burbs, especially in inner-ring or older suburbs, such as the Virginia-Highlands neighborhood in metro **Atlanta.** The **Williamsburg** neighborhood in **Brooklyn, New York**, is considered a hipster enclave, to the disgust of many long term residents.

HOA: Homeowners Association. A group of homeowners which manages (and in some respects governs) a housing development, in exchange for monthly dues paid by residents. **Example:** *An HOA can be considered a voluntary, additional layer of government, taken on by homeowners.*

H.O.A.-hole: An official of an **HOA** (Homeowners Association) who harshly enforces HOA rules. Sometimes described as an official on a "power trip."

hoarder: A person who collects an inordinate amount of possessions and/or refuse in his or her home.

hobo-sexual: 1. Someone who dresses sloppily. Especially someone who is oblivious to their sloppy and style-free dressing. **2.** Someone who *somehow* usually has a date or romantic partner despite their sloppy appearance.

See also: *style-free zone.*

hollow legs: Describes a person who can put away many drinks without appearing drunk. Also refers to someone who can eat generous portions of food.

Home Depot hookups: Term used by comedians for "liaisons" in storage sheds. These sheds can be found for sale in the parking lot of The Home Depot and other retailers. (But whose looking?)

homeschooled: Overused term to describe someone lacking in social skills.

hooch: Inferior alcohol or liquor, often illegally obtained or brewed in storage sheds.

Hooch, The: Nickname for the Chattahoochee River, which flows near **Atlanta, Georgia.**

"Hope you like dog hair.": Often unspoken slogan of those with shedding dogs when visitors arrive.

hot mess: A person or situation that is disorganized or untidy, yet is somehow interesting or attractive. ***Example:***

Sorority sister # 1: "He seems like sort of a hot mess."

Sorority sister # 2: "Well, you got the 'mess' part right."

See also: *attractive nuisance.*

hot snot: Vintage term used by kids and teens for those who think very highly of themselves.

HOV stand-ins: A passenger (or dummy made up to look like a passenger) riding in a car solely so the driver can use the HOV (high occupancy vehicle, or carpool) lane.

"How do you get...?": Common precursor to a cynical or snooty question. ***Example:***

Person # 1: "Well, I'm going to have a sumptuous meal at Denny's."

Person 2: "How do you get "sumptuous" out of Denny's?"

"How's that working out for you?": In suburbanese, a (usually) snarky question pointing out a bad decision. ***Example:***

Man at high school reunion: "A few years after high school, I decided to buy a Blockbuster video franchise."

Woman at reunion: "How's that working out for you?"

humble brag (humblebrag): Bragging but couching it in the form of modesty or even as misfortune. Commonly found on social media. One recent trend: to "apologize" for inventing something which may have been obnoxious, and thereby brag about your invention. ***Examples:*** *"I hate it when a movie producer offers you a huge movie deal, and you have to drop whatever you're doing."*

"Isn't it a pain when an Italian supermodel asks you out for the night, and you already have a date that evening?"

hurricane bait: A beachfront property.

- I -

"I am not part of this conversation.": Response used by suburbanites and others when quite pissed off.

IBM: Vintage snide slang among police officers referring to a member of organized crime. Stands for Italian businessman.

"I can wait.": Typical suburbanese retort, showing a lack of enthusiasm *Example:*

Boss: "I bet you can't wait to hear about my trip to Milwaukee."

Employee: "Uh, I can wait."

"I can't tell you how many times ...": An expression that can be straightforward or nuanced. If someone tells you "I can't tell you how many times it has rained in **Seattle**," this is a straightforward telling of much rain. Conversely, someone could say "I can't tell you how many times Phoebe helped wash the dishes." This could mean that Phoebe has never helped wash the dishes, hence there's "no telling."

ice cream truck: Ice cream delivering vehicle, which can bring mass excitement to neighbourhood kids in summertime. It's frowned upon to tell your little kids that when the ice cream truck plays music, that means that the truck is out of ice cream.

IDK: I don't know. Used in texts. Also a teen joke setup, as in: "What does IDK mean?"

"I'd rather have a root canal than...": A statement of severe disdain. *Example: "I'd rather have a root canal than meet with those H.O.A.-holes again."*

"If you see one, let me know.": Snarky comeback, usually directed toward blowhards. *Example:*

Dude at nightclub: "Have you ever dated a real *man?"*

Woman at nightclub: "No, but if you see one, let me know."

"I hope you're happy, too!": Cheeky response to a scolding.

*Example: Mom scolding a daughter: "You haven't helped clean this house one bit. I hope you're **happy!**"*

*Teenage daughter: "I hope **you're** happy **too, Mom!**"*

***IKEA Heights*:** Satire of soap operas filmed (without permission from IKEA) inside a suburban Los Angeles IKEA store. Episodes are available on YouTube and on star actor Randall Park's website called RandallParkPlace.com.

"I'll Venmo you.": The new "the check is in the mail." A convenient way for someone to stiff you.

"I'm just curious...": Expression often heard before someone asks you something they truly are dying to know about. "I'm just curious" is also often used as an intro for a **gotcha** question, in which the asker already knows the answer. **See also:** *gotcha question.*

imagineered: Term used in Disney circles to describe the blend of imagination and engineering used to create often amazing rides and resorts.

inadvertent: Unintended. Often used to describe unintentional harm.

in season: Polite term for female animals in heat.

in the zone: Crushing it or feeling it. Performing a task skillfully or being able to think clearly.

Example: Drunk teenager getting into the driver's seat: "Don't worry dudes, I'm in the zone!"

increasingly unstable: Useful, official-sounding term to describe a co-worker who gets on your nerves.

"Ink in your blood": Describes someone who cannot resist the temptation to write, or to work in journalism.

inner puppy: Term used to describe the basic emotional needs of the inner child, or inner puppy, of pet dogs.

innumeracy: The math(s) equivalent of illiteracy. A lack of understanding of math and by extension, economics. Much more common than illiteracy. **Example:**

Wife: "Okay, I'm off to buy a lottery ticket."

Husband, who is also an economics professor: "Hon, playing the lottery is a sign of innumeracy."

*Wife: "Hon, you can take your 'innumeracy' and **stick it!**"*

See also: *math(s).*

"Interesting": This can mean something is interesting, can politely be a way of saying something is uninteresting, or imply that someone or something is weird.

internet machine: Ha-ha term for a personal computer (PC) or laptop, especially when used by a tech-challenged person.

intrapreneur: Blend of "intra" and entrepreneur. A person within a company in charge of rolling out a new product or service.

Irish goodbye: Leaving a social event without saying goodbye or telling anyone you are leaving.

Irish Riviera: 1. The south shore area of **Boston, Massachusetts.** So named because of the many Irish American residents (and bars). **2.** Any coastal area with a prevalence of Irish ancestry folks. **See also:** *Deluxbury.*

Irish twins: Siblings born within twelve months of each other; "near twins."

-ish: Useful suffix indicating a "ballpark" figure that allows leeway for the habitually late.. ***Example:*** *"Let's meet at ten-ish."*

IT: Information Technology. In many suburban homes, the IT department is a teenager (or even a preteen).

"I think that's *awesome* when you think you're funny.": Typical sarcastic retort when someone is the butt of a joke.

- J -

Jake brake: A loud braking technique used on large trucks. Outlawed in some upscale cities because of the loud noise. Sounds like a truck engine repeatedly backfiring. *Example: If you see a sign noting "No Jake Brake," or "No Engine Brake," you know you're probably entering an upscale 'burb.*

James Blonde: A dimwitted and/or a plain-looking man with blonde hair.

janky: Shady, disreputable. Often refers to unreliable technology.

Jeremiah's Vanishing New York: Blog, website (vanishingnewyork.blogspot.com), and book chronicling the gradual disappearance of one-of-a-kind businesses and properties in metro **New York.** Affectionately written by Jeremiah Moss (his pen name), the blog laments the passing of old-school delicatessens and other mom-and-pop businesses. The "vanishing" properties are often replaced by expensive housing, chain retailers, or hipster cafés serving coffee in jam-jars. His book: *Vanishing New York: How a Great City Lost Its Soul.*

jerk-storing: Slang term for thinking of the perfect witty "comeback" just a moment too late. Named for a *Seinfeld* episode involving the ever-smooth character George Costanza. Also called "staircase wit," because you often think of the perfect answer on the stairs on the way out. Damn it! **See also:** *zinger.*

Jesus boots: Sandals, in Texas slang.

Jew-Bu (Jewish Buddhist): Friendly term for a Jewish person who has embraced the practices, meditation, and in some cases the beliefs of Buddhism. Among the many books to chronicle this is ABC newsman Dan Harris's 2014 memoir, *10% Happier: How I Tamed the Voice in*

My Head, Reduced Stress Without Losing My Edge, and Found Self-Help That Actually Works—A True Story.

jingle mail: Term used to describe house keys that arrive in the mail at a mortgage company when a borrower walks away from their home (and away from the mortgage debt).

job slave: A person who feels compelled to stay at his or her job, usually for economic reasons. Also refers to a person who is afraid to abandon his or her employer's health insurance because of a "pre-existing" illness. **See also:** *golden handcuffs.*

John Daly: An Arnold Palmer (iced tea and lemonade) with vodka added. Named for US golfer John Daly, who enjoyed this drink at clubhouses, and pretty much anywhere else.

Jokeland: Nickname for **Oakland, California**, considered a suburb, or **superburb**, of **San Francisco**.

JOMO: Joy of missing out. Describes the sensation of relief when someone no longer feels compelled to frequently "check in" regarding email and social media sites.

julep: A cocktail with flavorful herbs, especially mint. In medieval times, a julep was a potion of sweet juices masking harsh medicines. From the Arabic word for "rose water."

- K -

Keep Austin Weird: Slogan of many in **Austin, Texas.**

Keep Calm and Carry On: Powerful but understated message from the British government to citizens during World War II. Considered a hallmark of British determination. The slogan was nearly forgotten until a bookstore owner in **Northumberland, England**, in 2000 discovered one of the few remaining original posters of this message while sorting used books. The owner of Barter Books displayed the poster near his cash register. So many folks asked about it that he decided to print and sell copies, setting off a marketing phenomenon. "Keep Calm" coffee mugs and T-shirts now seemingly number in the millions.

See also: *power through it.*

Kentucky: Could be considered, to a certain extent, a suburban state. Features suburbs and the largest airport of the **Cincinnati, Ohio,** area.

See also: *bourbon, Pennsyltucky.*

(The) kids' table: Time-honored tradition at gatherings such as Christmas or Thanksgiving in which an "overflow" dining table is set up for kids.

kirk: Scottish word for "church." A term also used by some Americans.

Kissimmee, Florida: Area on the outskirts of **Orlando** with a chuckle-inducing name.

Kool-Aid drinker: A person who is overly loyal to an employer or other entity. In workplace circles, a person who parrots the employer's talking points is called a Kool-Aid drinker. ***Example:*** *After that last sales meeting, I think Dwight earned the "Kool-Aid Drinker of the Year" award.*

kvetch: A Yiddish word that means to complain habitually. Nearly rhymes with another word for complaining.

- L -

labelscar, label scar: Also called a "logo scar." The mark left on an abandoned retail store after the sign on the facade is removed. Similar to the spot on your wrist that does not tan when your wear a wristwatch (or a Fitbit). Label scars can linger for decades as a sort of urban fossil. ***Example:***

Mall shopper # 1: "How did you know there used to be a Sears store here?"

Mall shopper # 2: "Saw the label scar."

labradoodles: The result of Labrador retrievers and poodles breeding. These handsome and playful dogs are popular in the burbs and elsewhere.

Labyrinth, The: A series of tunnels under **Minneapolis, Minnesota.** The Labyrinth was little known until recently gaining attention as a destination for **"urban explorers."** The tunnels are from abandoned sand mines, pipelines, sewers, and cellars of abandoned breweries. Well covered in the book *Unruly Places: Lost Spaces, Secret Cities, and Other Inscrutable Geographies* by Alastair Bonnett.

lackanookie: A dry spell with little or no bedroom activities.

lad lit: Books aimed at teenage boys and men. A parallel to chick lit.

(The) Land Before Avocado: Wistful book by Richard Glover about the Australia of the 1960s and '70s. Glover rues white-bread living but longs for times when "nearly everyone" could afford to buy a home.

landfill: The politically correct term for a city or county dump, usually built at the edge of a county. If a county is rectangular, the landfill is often placed in the county's corner.

Example: *Most suburbanites aim to live somewhere between downtown and the county landfill.* **See also: Astroturfing, county line, NIMBY, PIITBY.**

landmine: Slang for dog excrement or other hazards hidden within grassy lawns, now lying in wait for a pedestrian.

landscraper: Derisive term for landscaping crews, especially those with leaf blowers.

"Later, hater!": Dismissal used by teens and kids.

lawns: A grassy area often surrounding a home. According to some estimates, lawns in the United States occupy 50,000 square miles, an area nearly the size of **Pennsylvania! See also: *synthetic lawn.***

(*The*) *Lay of the Land:* Prize–winning novel from 2006 by Richard Ford. A midlife New Jersey realtor decides to *actually* start scratching off bucket list activities, both wholesome and otherwise. High jinks ensue. **See also: *Wealth Belt (New Jersey).***

leafy: Semi-mandatory journalists' term for a green suburb with many trees and gardens.

less than ideal: Suburban term for a shitty situation.

"Let us know how that works out.": Suburbanese expression that implies someone is going to be on their own if they engage in a proposed endeavor. Roughly translates to "That's the shittiest idea I've ever heard."

lexicographer: A writer of dictionaries. A harmlessdrudge. **See also: *backronym.***

Lexus lane: A toll-charging express lane, or premium lane, on a public highway, used by those who are wealthy, boastful or, sometimes, genuinely in a hurry.

libraries: A sort of shrine to books and learning where silence must be observed—or is supposed to be observed—while one reads. Could also be viewed as a sort of well-organized, state-supported study hall for grown-ups, in which librarians are like school teachers watching over the "adults."

life: In a quip attributed to alternative health guru Deepak Chopra, life is "a sexually-transmitted terminal disease." Perhaps better described as a condition or state, but not as a disease. John Lennon said (actually sang) that life is what happens while you are making other plans.

lit: 1. Awesome, excellent. A term used by teens, and occasionally by their parents, to the disgust of teens. **2.** Wasted, drunk, high. **3.** Seems oddly placed alongside the previous definitions, but, here goes: literature. Especially "lit" class in high school or college. (Warning: this entry may trigger a flood of memories for those long-graduated from college.)

litterlout: British term for a litterbug. A problem in the burbs, as elsewhere.

Little Saigon: Term for the large concentration of Vietnamese Americans in the **Orange County** suburbs near Los Angeles, California. Interestingly, Little Saigon is only about a fifteen-minute drive west of Disneyland. *See also:* **Orange Curtain.**

LMFAO: Laughing my f**king ass off. A frequent note in emails and in texts.

loafers: Relaxing, casual footwear, once a mainstay in the burbs. Ideal for those who don't know how to (or are too lazy to) tie their shoes.

lollipop lady: In the UK, a school crossing-guard. So called because the "Stop" sign when held up resembles a lollipop. A common sight in the suburbs, where they are loved by parents, and sometimes hated by passing drivers.

Los Alamos, New Mexico: A city on a mesa over 6,000 feet high. Truly a "city on a hill." The town is thirty-three miles northwest of, and is an exurb of, **Santa Fe.**

lozenge lane: A special-purpose lane on a highway, such as an **HOV lane.** Such lanes are marked with a lozenge or diamond-shaped symbol. **See also:** *HOV lane*, *Lexus lane.*

LSD: Lake Shore Drive, one of **Chicagoland's** most famous roadways.

lurker: Someone who observes but does not post or otherwise participate on a social media site. Can be either harmless or a bit creepy.

- M -

ma'aming: Unjustifiably and irritatingly calling a slightly older woman "ma'am.

Example: Clothing store clerk: "I'm sorry, Ma'am, we can't accept a return of that dress."

Thirty-something customer: "Stop ma'aming me! I'm only a few years older than you!"

See also: *sirring.*

MacArthur Park: A park in suburban LA near downtown. Notable as the place in which a love-sick songwriter witnessed somebody leaving a cake out on a picnic table during a sudden rainstorm. Pop music would never be the same, as the song *MacArthur Park* was jotted down soon afterward.

Mahalo: "Thank you" in Hawaiian.

Make it happen, Cap'n!: Friendly expression of encouragement.

malarkey: rubbish, nonsense. Many view this as an Irish expression, but it's of uncertain origin. Some say it comes from the Greek word *malakas,* which means "stupid," or "jerk." Maybe the dad in the movie *My Big Fat Greek Wedding*—who claimed that all words have a "Greek root"—was right after all!

mallmanac: Map and retail guide near the entrance to a shopping mall that tells you, somewhat obviously, that "you are here." Word blend of "mall" and "almanac," this term was noted on the website **Deadmalls.com. See also: *Deadmalls.com.***

mall rat: A person who spends excessive amounts of time at shopping malls, as immortalised in the 1995 movie *Mallrats* during which two of the main characters assault the mall's Easter Bunny due to a misunderstanding. **See also:** *desert rat, gym rat.*

man bag: A murse or male purse, often seen as a sign of metrosexuality. **See also:** *messenger bag.*

man bun: A hairstyle popular among men wearing a man bun, though not as popular (some say) among those viewing the man bun. Man buns have increased in popularity, along with yoga. A new development is the hipster double bun in which a primary bun is topped by a second miniature bun. When a large dude wears a man bun, he seems to vaguely resemble a *sumo* wrestler.

man cave: Male retreat or sanctuary in a home, often in a specially equipped garage or basement. A place in which menfolk needn't worry about female questioning or supervision. Reporters say the term "man cave" originated in the 1992 best-selling book *Men Are from Mars, Women Are from Venus* by John Gray. **See also:** *Garage Mahal: she shed; study.*

mansion: An exceedingly large and expensive residence. Rarely will you hear the owners of such a home refer to it as a mansion. **Example:** *"No way will I ask the plumber to fix the sink at my 'mansion.' Then he will charge me double. Or triple."*

mansionette (American): Synonymous with *McMansion*: An oversized house in comparison to:

- the surrounding homes
- the lot on which it stands
- the financial resources of the home buyer

mansionette (British): A flat (apartment) of two or more stories.

mansplanation: An over-explanation by a man, usually directed toward a woman. A "blowhard" treatment. Often involves supposedly technical subjects.

mantuary: A man's refuge or sanctuary. **See also: man cave, study.**

maphead: Someone who takes great pleasure in maps, geography, and atlases.

marijuana dispensaries: Pot-selling outlets that are often low-key but present in many states where marijuana has been legalized. The outlets often feature green-colored signs (or so the author has been told), and will often be labeled **CBD,** or **MMJ. See also:** *budtender, CBD.*

mash-up: Term for a blend of unlikely genres. A typical mash-up is Jane Austen novels and zombie themes. Result? The 2016 film *Pride and Prejudice and Zombies.*

maths: British version of the word "math."

Example: If you say the word "math" around Brits, you will likely hear a reflexively added "S" sound.

"May I be excused?": Polite expression still heard at some suburban dinner tables when a child has finished eating.

May the 4th: Star Wars Day. (As often explained, the name sounds like "May the force" as in "May the force be with you.") **See also:** *Wookieepedia.*

"May the forest be with you.": Good wishes from Nature lovers. This slogan is seen on bumper stickers (especially on Prius vehicles). Also a name given to events promoting tree planting, many of which are on **May the 4th. See also:** *Vitamin N.*

McMansion: An oversized suburban home. **See also:** *mansionette.*

McSandwiched: Condition in which a modest home is sandwiched between two oversized **McMansions.** Not a new condition. In F. Scott Fitzgerald's 1920s novel *The Great Gatsby,* Nick Carraway describes renting a small cottage on **Long Island** between two mansions. A term originated in *Suburban Dictionary.*

meatloaf line: A term coined by writer David Brooks of the *New York Times.* Refers to the transition zone where affluent suburbs fade into the countryside. Inside the line, trendy suburbanites rarely eat meatloaf. Outside the line, meatloaf is still a staple.

"Meh": Expression indicating that a subject at hand is mediocre at best. *Example:*

Diner # 1: "How did you like that Vietnamese restaurant called Mekong that you went to?"

Diner # 2: "Meh."

menoporsche: The male equivalent of menopause involving a midlife crisis. Trying to regain youthfulness, middle-agers will often buy an "impressive" sports car, such as a Porsche.

messenger bag: A more acceptable term to some for a *murse* (male purse or man's purse). **See also:** *murse.*

Methademic: **1.** A song by Ozzy Osbourne's Black Sabbath band about a meth addiction "epidemic." **2.** Informal term for the scourge of meth addiction that swept through many areas (including the suburbs) in the late 1990s and early 2000s. Still a problem today.

mews: British term for a carriage house, stables, or a garage. Also refers to such a building that has been converted to a home. TV reporters in May 2018 complimented the Royal Mews for the impressive horses and carriage that whisked away newlyweds Prince Harry and Meghan Markle.

Michigan left: Alternative method of turning left in auto traffic: turning right, and later doing a U-turn when it's (hopefully) safe to do so. Many roadways in Michigan provide U-turn "turnouts."

miffed: Angered or pissed off.

minimally exceptional: Not that bright. Could for instance be used to describe a **James Blonde.**

Minnesota nice: Often-observed quality of Minnesotans, including friendliness and patience (in some cases, at least). *See also: The Labyrinth (Minneapolis).*

Mississippi search warrant: Police slang for a battering ram used to knock down a suspect's door (sometimes without a search warrant, in police lore).

"mmm, bye!": Utterance used in phone conversations by control freaks or Type A personalities to "wrap up" a phone call. *Example: Newspaper reporter: "Hey, can I ask you another question?"*

HOA official, caught with his hand in the cookie jar: "Mmmm, bye."

mofo: Shorthand for mother f**ker. Usually used in a friendly or joking way.

***Money Pit, The*: 1.** Popular 1980s movie starring Tom Hanks and Shelley Long about the pitfalls of remodeling a home. Now a common term for any purchase that has led to a series of renovations. **2.** Popular US radio show about home remodeling.

monkey mind: Buddhist (and Yoga-related) term for someone prone to worrying or vain thoughts.

monsoon: Rainy season experienced in the second half of the summer in the south-western US or elsewhere. Some note that the Southwest has two summers: a dry first half and a humid second half. **See also:** *nonsoon.*

moonscape (also: **moonscrape**): An area that has been cleared (or scraped) for a housing project but was then left bare. Often occurs when a developer runs out of funding after clearing a property, leaving a "moonscape."

more chins than Chinatown: Old-school term for a double (or more) chin.

"More tea, Vicar?": Mostly British expression used to restore polite conversation flow after someone, um, farts. (A vicar is a parish pastor.)

moving right along: An expression encouraging someone to carry on with "the show" or with chit chat, after an awkward moment. **See also:** *More tea, Vicar?*

murse: A "man purse." Sometimes more sympathetically called a European carry-all or **messenger bag. Example:** *In a* Seinfeld *TV show episode, Jerry Seinfeld indignantly called his murse a "European carry-all."*

musical chairs: Term for simultaneously selling a house and attempting to buy a replacement home (perhaps an "upgrade") in a hot market. The seller may pay a dear price for the new home, if one can be found.

MWAH!: Kissing sound used in text messages, and also by the pretentious as they air kiss one another.

- N -

naan: Scrumptious flaky fresh bread served at Indian (south-Asian) restaurants, increasingly common in the burbs.

nagware: Annoying e-reminders or pop-ups nagging someone to take care of this or that e-chore.

nanobrewery: A brewery that is even smaller than most microbreweries.

nano-influencer: A person with a small but devoted following in a narrow field of interest. An example might be a person who blogs about a neighborhood and the characters therein, such as: the **lollipop lady, the crazy cat lady,** and the perhaps frowned-upon neighbors who built a **Garage Mahal.**

nanomanage: A step further than micromanaging in which a manager intensely over-supervises employees. A business world parallel to the "helicopter parent."

nappy: British term for diapers.

Nappy Valley: A neighborhood with many babies and toddlers. Named for the British word for diapers.

Nature trail: A trail of belly hair that leads from the belly button down toward the private parts.

neat: Whiskey or other liquor served straight. *"I'll have a whiskey, neat."*

"Nerd alert!": Playful notice given around nerdy behavior.

nerd neck: A hunched-over or tilted neck from too much staring at e-devices. Also called iHunch or text neck.

nerdvana: Any situation that is appealing to "nerds."

Example: "You're doing some process mapping this weekend? Nerdvana! Can I join in?"

Netfish and chill: Slogan of those who enjoy fishing, a play on **Netflix and chill.** Seen on T-shirts and bumper stickers.

Netflix and chill: 1. Relaxing at home with streaming movies and TV. **2.** A euphemism for going to someone's place for sexual activity. The double meaning can lead to embarrassing mix ups.

NEV: (neighborhood electric vehicle): A golf cart purposely built for use off the golf course. Especially common in retirement communities in **Florida** and elsewhere. A sort of grandma's Tesla.

New Jersey: Mid-Atlantic state in which suburbs of both **New York City** and **Philadelphia** seem to predominate. *An old quip: What are the largest cities in New Jersey? New York and Philadelphia.*

New Yorican: A New Yorker of Puerto Rican background.

nibling, niblings: A catchall term for nieces and/or nephews.

"Nice app!": A compliment for an app, or a nice rear end. **Example:** *As the Uber driver walked off and Phoebe watched him from behind, she blurted out: "Nice app!"*

nillionaire: Someone who lives the lifestyle of a rich person but has little money of his or her own. A blend of "nil" and "millionaire." Especially refers to someone in debt or someone who "married rich." Can also refer to someone who has repeatedly filed for bankruptcy, but *some-*

how continues to live the life of a rich person. Can you think of any examples? **See also: *struck oil at the altar.***

NINJA loan: Notorious loans issued during the height of the 2004–2006 housing bubble. A near-acronym that signifies a loan to someone with "no income, no job, no assets."

"No glove, no love": Oft-heard notice of no relations without a condom.

non-felines: Term used by cat lovers when referring to dogs.

nonrenew: Rather cynical term used by insurance companies that effectively means that your homeowner's insurance policy has been canceled.

nonsoon: Slang term for a "rainy" season or **monsoon** (in the Southwest US) that ultimately yields little rain. A drought. **See also: *monsoon.***

"No offense, but": A sentence introduction that seems to make the world stand still, as you wait to hear what comes next. Bad news (or a stupid opinion, at least) usually follows. The teller may be sincere in claiming "no offense," or may be eager to offend.

Example: *Karaoke singer # 1: "No offense, but your rendition of My Way was terrible."*

Karaoke singer # 2: "No offense, but you dress like a hobo-sexual."

noogie: Playful (or bullying) maneuver during which someone's head of hair is rubbed forcefully with the knuckles. Often done while the recipient is in a headlock.

"**No pressure, but...**": Ironic expression in suburbanese that actually means "I'm pressuring you" for a certain outcome or result.

normal college: Term used in the early 1900s for a college that trains school teachers. More than a few towns and neighborhoods are thus named. Examples include: **1. Normal, Illinois. 2. Normaltown,** a neighborhood of **Athens, Georgia**, near the University of Georgia.

not enough ponies: An underpowered vehicle, which is insufficient to allow you to overtake someone else's "wagon". **See also:** *comparisonitis.*

not enough steaks in the freezer: Insufficient funds for a desired lifestyle. *Example:*

Neighbor # 1: "I heard Peggy from down the street ran out on her husband Al. Why was that?"

Neighbor # 2: "Not enough steaks in the freezer."

"**Not tonight, dear**": Phrase often heard in suburban bedrooms.

"**Not working for me**": Suburbanese way of informing someone that a situation sucks, without getting into any details.

noun pile-up: An over-use of nouns as modifiers in a term or sentence. *Example:*

Q.: "So, how did you like your stay at Eagle Mountain Lake State Park Lodge?"

A.: "Whaat?"

NSFW: Not safe for work. Indicates an email or website that should *not* be viewed at work. A consideration for those who care about propriety, and also for those who care about their jobs.

Nutella: 1. Nickname for a crazy-acting female. **2.** A "chocolate and hazelnut" sandwich spread popular in suburban kitchens. (The main ingredients of Nutella are actually sugar and palm oil. When the marketing department gets hold of something, **stuff happens**.)

- O -

"Oatmilk": Charming outcome when little toddlers try to say "oatmeal."

(The) OC: 1. Orange County, California, a suburban area south of Los Angeles. Home to Disneyland. Famous (or infamous) as the home of the reality TV show *Real Housewives of Orange County.* Features one of the largest Vietnamese populations in the western hemisphere. OC residents stridently proclaim that the county is "not part of LA." **See also:** *Orange Curtain.* **2. Oklahoma City, Oklahoma.**

off-boarding: Business-speak for dumping an employee or a customer.

off-grid: Avoiding conventional utilities such as power companies in favor of self-sufficiency via generators, solar panels, or other devices. The Amish are well known for often remaining off-grid. The term off-grid also describes a person who rarely (or never) subscribes to any service that requires disclosure of a physical address, possibly for nefarious reasons, possibly for hyper-concerns regarding privacy.

"Oh, OK.": Expression of surprise, or feigned surprise, after a disclosure. Can be used to stall for time during a difficult conversation.

Old Sod, The: The "old land." Reverent name for someone's native country. Often used for England, Ireland, or Scotland, but this term can be applied to any "homeland."

on everything but roller skates: Heavily medicated.

Opa!: Greek expression of excitement, often heard at parties and celebrations.

OPA: Other people's agenda. A term used to describe distractions or "time sucks." Especially applies to distractions such as spam or clickbait.

optionaire: Someone who is rich (on paper, at least) due to lucrative stock options, usually from his or her employer.

Orange Curtain: The border between **Orange County** and **Los Angeles County** in Southern California. The term is a play on the infamous Iron Curtain (which once divided free nations and Communist nations in Europe). Locals say that Orange County is far more conservative (and not nearly as exciting?) as nearby Los Angeles.

organic foods: Category of food that is produced without synthetic chemicals. **Example:** *What came first? The free-range chicken or the organic egg?*

"our space": Amusing pronunciation of "outer space" sometimes used by grade school kids, after a science class.

outdoorsmen: Snarky term for the homeless.

- P -

pain in the neck: Suburbanese for "pain in the ass."

Parakeets, keets: A play on *Parrot Heads*, devoted fans of singer Jimmy Buffett. Younger fans of Buffett—or the children of Buffett fans—are known as Parakeets.

Parrot Head (Parrothead): Devoted fans of singer Jimmy Buffett.

patio party: A party held by trespassers on the patio of a beach house while the owners are away.

payback: Returning a "favor." Also, what the universe sometimes gives you in return for a questionable deed.

peanut: Nickname for babies, toddlers, and pets.

PEBCAK: Tech-support expression in the workplace meaning "problem exists between chair and keyboard"—in other words, the user is an idiot. IT staff adopted the practice of snooty acronyms from doctors who coined similar terms for patients such as AALFD, meaning "Another A**hole Looking For Drugs".

Pennsyltucky: Sometimes good-natured, sometimes snide term for rural **Pennsylvania.** To some, this is any part of the state outside of metro **Philadelphia** or **Pittsburgh.** A blend of "Pennsylvania" and "Kentucky." Historians say it's not just a funny nickname. In the tumultuous early days of the US, many Pennsylvanians moved from the Quaker State to Kentucky.

Penta: Supplement to *Barron's* weekly finance newspaper aimed at penta-millionaires: those worth at least $5 million.

period rush: A rush or feeling of euphoria felt by those in a historical re-enactment, such as a (U.S.) Civil War battle. Participants claim they suddenly feel as though they *are in* the period being depicted. Noted and claimed by more than a few re-enactors. Perhaps akin to a *deja vu* experience. *Example: Josh claimed that as the horses galloped by and the bugles blared, he was suddenly swept up in a **period rush.***

See also: *cosplay.*

pescetarian (pescatarian): A person who does not eat mammals or other meat but does eat fish. One of many "levels" of vegetarianism.

"picking up what you're putting down": An expression that signifies "I understood what you meant." *Example:*

Jerry: *"We're flying to LA on Friday."*

Elaine: *"Okay."*

Jerry: *"Wait, I meant Saturday."*

Elaine: *"It's okay. I was picking up what you were putting down."*

PIITBY: Put it in *their* backyard. Aggressive term used by residents involved in city planning decisions. A step farther than **Not in my backyard (NIMBY)**. *Example: When asked to pick between two proposed landfill sites, residents nearly always pick the site furthest from their home: classic PIITBY.*

Pill Hill: Seasoned term for a neighborhood or burb featuring a concentration of doctors and/or hospitals. A sort of "scrub-burb."

Pine Curtain: Imaginary dividing line between woodsy East Texas and the much drier West Texas.

ping: To send someone a text or email.

pingry: When a busy person receives distracting pings (texts or emails) and becomes angry. Word blend of "ping" and "angry." **See also: *JO-MO; hangry.***

pipe smoker: Car salesman slang for a shopper who remains noncommittal and shows no enthusiasm for any vehicles, but continues to look at car models.

pissin' match: A loud argument or a vengeful dispute.

Example: An old country expression warns, "Don't get in a pissin' match with a polecat."

pity party: A period of indulging in sorrow after a disappointment. Sometimes connotes a cathartic experience, and often involves eating ice cream directly from the carton.

pizza model: City planning term describing how metro areas often grow in an outward pattern with several new "downtowns" dotting the "pie" surface, resembling a pepperoni pizza.

place dropping: To casually mention in conversation the name of a place you've visited (or claim to have visited) in the hopes of impressing someone. Similar to "name dropping." ***Example: Wow, this Nutella sandwich tastes like the one I had in Prague last summer.***

plastic surgery: A favorite pastime of patients as well as doctors in suburbia. Also, apparently the main source of advertising for suburban magazines.

plate smashing, plate breaking: A demonstration of wealth, sometimes seen at Greek weddings. **See also: *Opa!***

platonic: A relationship or friendship that is not sexual or physical. ***Example: Some say "platonic" is one of the most depressing words in the dictionary.***

polenta: Italian-style grits, popular in some suburban households and restaurants.

pool pirates: Someone who sneaks into a hotel pool or resort pool while not a guest of the hotel.

poppy-seed bagels, poppy-seed muffins: Baked goods that are sometimes used as an excuse for failing drug tests in the workplace. Or so a friend of the author claims.

porch pirates: Thieves who steal deliveries from your front porch or stoop.

"power through it": To persevere over setbacks, aided by determination. Can also refer to ignoring your taste buds and "powering through" a bland or unpleasant meal. *Example:*

Q.: "How were you able to finish binge-watching all those Keeping Up with the Kardashians *episodes?"*

A.: "We just powered through it."

See also: *Keep calm and carry on.*

prairie-dogging: Standing up to peer (at your peers) over your cubicle in the workplace.

pre-cleaning: Light cleaning done before a cleaning person arrives to avoid embarrassment over a messy home. Some insist on this practice, others claim this is border-line "cuckoo."

preppers: Sometimes called "survivalists," those who prep for emergencies such as extreme weather or for some sort of collapse of social order. Prepping can include stockpiling food or building some sort of shelter. **See also:** *off-grid.*

presenteeism: The opposite of absenteeism. Condition in which a co-worker rarely uses vacation or sick days; or simply spends too much time at work. Usually considered unhealthy behavior. In some countries, presenteeism means staying at work after you've done your duties but waiting on your boss to leave first. Notably, some employers have ditched so-called "Perfect Attendance" awards in recent years. **See also:** *skate.*

professorial: Of or relating to a university professor. Seeming "professor-like" in appearance or behavior. ***Example:***

Monica: *"Wearing that tweed blazer and glasses, you sure do look professorial."*

Ross: *"Thanks ... I think."*

See also: *Freeway Professor.*

"Promise?": Sometimes sarcastic retort, frequently heard in suburbanese. ***Example:****Mr.: "This is the last time I will try to fix anything in this house!"*

Mrs.: "Promise?"

pushback: 1. Resistance to a proposal, especially in the workplace. **2.** "Pushing back" an airplane from its berth at an airport as part of the departure process.

- Q -

quarter-life crisis: Crisis often impacting twenty-somethings when they begin to take on adult responsibilities but are still teenagers in spirit. Also called a "mid-youth crisis."

Queen City: Nickname for a city that is a state's largest but is not the capital. Possibly an allusion to the game of Chess, in which the queen is viewed as the most powerful piece. Example cities, in no particular order, include **Anchorage, Alaska; Burlington, Vermont; Charlotte, North Carolina, and Detroit, Michigan.** (Okay, these examples were in alphabetical order.)

Queen of Versailles, The: Absorbing 2012 documentary by Lauren Greenfield. The film depicts Jackie and David Siegel, then owners of a massive timeshare resort company. Viewers follow the Siegels as they build their private home—called Versailles—near **Orlando, Florida.** When completed, it was one of the largest homes in the US. The Siegels faced a crisis as the real estate market tumbled in 2008 and faced possibly losing their home. Spoiler alert: the couple was able to keep their home after an arduous financial battle—although this is not known and therefore not disclosed at the time of the filming.

quirkiness in the burbs: A time-honored tradition. Denotes a person who is different in an awkward but harmless, perhaps even charming, way. Every *cul-de-sac* is expected to have at least one quirky (dare we say eccentric?) resident or family. **HOAs** aren't generally impressed by quirkiness. **See also:** *HOAs; H.O.A.- hole.*

- R -

ramp lizard: A person who socializes with and watches hang gliders, but does not actually glide or participate. So called because they hang out on the launching ramp.

Rancho Relaxo: Amusing name for "resorts" in both fact and fiction.

1. Resort featured on *The Simpsons* TV show. In an episode of the third season, Marge seeks refuge from Homer at "Rancho Relaxo."

2. A real-life animal sanctuary in **New Jersey**. "Residents" include horses, goats, chickens, and cats. http://www.ranchorelaxonj.org/animals/

3. Name used by *Parks and Recreation* TV show's Nick Offerman for one of his earlier homes in suburban **Los Angeles**.

"rearrange your face": To beat up someone.

recluse: Personality type that seems to be a fixture in some neighborhoods: a person who lives in near seclusion. In a typical scenario, a person lives only three or four doors from you, but you see this person only in occasional glimpses. With the surge in delivery services of daily needs such as prepared meals, it will become ever easier to "become" a recluse. **See also:** *Grey Gardens.*

Redneck Riviera: The **Florida Panhandle** coast in the US. The **Myrtle Beach, South Carolina,** area is sometimes also called this.

reeferendum: A referendum concerning the legalization of pot.

REI: Outdoor gear and clothing retailer, officially Recreational Equipment Inc. Organized as a co-op. Popular in suburban shopping areas. *Example: When visiting **REI**, you notice the employees seem reassuringly healthy and wholesome in appearance.*

religious experience: Term used metaphorically to describe an amazing or enthralling experience. Also describes an experience that results in a lifestyle change. Sometimes called a "peak experience." ***Example:*** *Looking back on it, my first time visiting **Hawaii** was sort of a religious experience.*

repurpose: 1. To find a new purpose for an item instead of discarding it: a popular hipster activity, for instance when old jamjars are used to serve drinks. Also common in the suburbs, as in the conversion of old wooden pallets into planters. **2.** To have a sex change.

restraining order: A court order to protect a person in a situation involving possible violence, harassment, or stalking. In escalated feuds between neighbors, one or both parties may seek restraining orders. ***Example:***

Neighbor # 1: "That asshole down the street got a restraining order on me!"

Neighbor # 2: "Welcome to the neighborhood."

See also: "sue".

retail therapy: Using shopping as a diversion (dare we say as a treatment?) for anxiety or depression. Rarely a cure for money worries.

reverse diet: Term for easing your way out of a dietary regimen and gradually returning to normal food intake. **See also: *bro science.***

reverse greeter: Employee at a retail store that eyeballs you or checks your receipt when you leave. **See also: *Costcop.***

reverse harem: Genre of fiction in which a female lead character has three or more men who are in love with her.

reverse hike: A hike that begins at a relatively high elevation, descends, and then returns. Hikers who walk from a canyon rim (canyon top) to the bottom and back are reverse hikers.

reverse satire: 1. A comedy in which roles are reversed. An example is the popular movie *Freaky Friday*, in which the children take on the roles of the parents. **2.** A subtle form of comedy in which a more subdued work (a book or film) satirizes an over-the-top earlier comedy with understated treatment.

Example: *Lit professor talking to students: "Can anyone here think of an example of a reverse satire?"*

Suburban Dictionary *author: "Well, now that you mention it ..."*

(The) rez: Indian reservations. Once viewed as far from big cities, suburbs now lap at the edge of these Native American reserves in many areas. Often home to casinos and other attractions. **Example:**

College student # 1: "Where's Achak? Haven't seen him lately."

College student # 2: "He spends his summers on the rez."

ringing endorsement: Term often used sarcastically to denote a dubious honor. **Example:**

Chandler: "That place is the best sushi restaurant in Des Moines." Joey: "There's a ringing endorsement."

roach coach: A food truck.

Rock Hudson: A golf shot that looked straight, but wasn't.

roof rats: Shyster roofing contractors. **See also: *storm chasers.***

rooftop garden: Weeds growing on a rooftop or in gutters due to infrequent cleaning.

- S -

sancho: Latino slang for a woman's illicit lover.

sandominium: Camping out on a beach. Sometimes refers to a homeless person camping on a beach.

San Pornando Valley: Ha-ha name for the San Fernando Valley suburbs, north of Los Angeles. The Valley has more than its share of both "legitimate" and porno movie studios. **See also:** *Silicone Valley.*

Santarchy: A recent Christmas "tradition" in which a large group of revelers dons Santa Claus garb. The group then engages in events such as pub crawls. Popular in cities including New York and San Francisco. A word blend of "Santa" and "anarchy." Also called "SantaCon." Some say this started as a protest against Christmastime consumerism.

savage: Teen term for someone who is snarky or skilled in verbal self-defense. Can be a term of praise. ***Example:***

Jess: "If I had a face like Brad's I'd sue my parents."

Ella: "Savage!"

schadenfreude: German term that translates to "damage joy." It's a pleasure gained from witnessing another's troubles.

Example: *Watching the lawyer's Maserati being towed away, I felt a touch of **schadenfreude**. Wait, make that a **boat load** of schadenfreude.*

scrape: Completely removing a home from a parcel of land; "scraping" the home. An example is provided by Elin Nordegren, the ex-wife of golf champion Tiger Woods. She scraped their former home after the couple separated. She then built a new home on the same lot in suburban **Orlando, Florida.** The first step in building a *McMansion* in many cases is scraping the existing (often quite adequate) home from the lot.

scrum: 1. Business term for a rapid, teamwork effort at innovation. For many years "scrum" referred to software writing. **2.** Formation of rugby players, akin to American football's "offensive line." **3.** Ha-ha term in the UK for the shoppers who gather to wait for reduced items to be put out at the end of a supermarket's day, then pounce to grab the best bargains.

scrummy: Food that is scrumptious and yummy.

scrumpets: 1. Scrumptious crumpets. Crumpets are griddle cakes, quite popular in Britain. Crumpet is also slang for an attractive woman.

sentence finishing: Interrupting and finishing someone else's sentence. An irritating habit that often derails a conversation. In a marriages, a potentially fatal habit. The most irritating form of sentence finishing: when someone interrupts and botches a joke you've been setting up.

serial monogamist: A person who does not necessarily cheat on romantic partners, but frequently changes ("ditches") partners.

shaken, not stirred: Time-honored term referring to a subtle drink mixing method.

"Shall I notify the media?": Sarcastic retort when someone gives you information that you don't care about.

Example:

Bank customer at teller counter: "I want to open an account."

Bank teller: "Wow! Shall I notify the media?"

shamployee: A phenomenon noticed when someone has been laid off or fired, and continues to dress for work and leave home at the same time every day. There appears to be a spectrum ranging from those who simply want to maintain a routine to those who are playing the part.

she-shed, she shed: Considered the female's answer to **man caves.** She-sheds are a sort of escape pod for women, often in a converted garden shed, in which they can pursue their own pursuits, which are often much more wholesome than those that are typical in man caves, in peace and solitude.

shill: Someone who poses as a customer or audience member, but is actually an employee. Once common in nightclubs and casinos, it's reported shills are still found at "get rich quick" presentations, pretending to be eager prospects.

ship: Teen and young adult term for relationships. This term is also used to convey a feeling that two characters in a book or movie should or will eventually get together. **Example:** *"I am totally shipping Princess Leia and Han Solo."*

ship name: A mashed up name of two romantic partners. An example is Jennifer Lopez + Ben Affleck = Bennifer.

shitsuckers: Construction worker slang for truck drivers who maintain and drain out portable toilets.

shoplifting center: Ha-ha name for shopping centers.

shrink: A psychiatrist. *Example: I just found out my shrink is seeing a shrink.*

shrinkflation: A mostly British term for shrinking quantities when buying items at the supermarket. Common in the US are cereal boxes with much less cereal but with a price that's the same or higher. Also common are foil bags of coffee, which have shrunk first from sixteen ounces to twelve ounces and are now sometimes ten ounces. After a period of shrinkflation, the manufacturer often reintroduces a special "maxi size" option at twice the price, which usually turns out to be the same size as the original packaging.

"Shut the front door!": Suburbanese for "Shut the f**k up!"

sibs: siblings. **See also:** *Niblings.*

sick: Excessive. Impressive. (Probably an example of the kind of teen slang that makes an adult look foolish, should they attempt to use it.) *Example: Dude, that five-car garage is sick!*

sighting: Term used to imply that when someone or something is "sighted," it's a remarkable event. One example might be a sasquatch sighting. *Example:*

Diner at a restaurant: "Jesus! Our dinner is taking forever. Has anyone seen the waiter?"

Fellow diner: "Yes! I just had a waiter sighting!"

signs, bogus: The practice of placing an unauthorized sign in a location and attempting to make the sign look official. For example, a homeowner might place an official-looking "No Parking" sign along the street in front of their home. In the UK people often erect similar signs reading "Polite Notice" assuming that many motorists will misread this as "Police Notice."

silent generation: The name given by many to the generation in between the World War II generation and the **baby boomers.** The group was born mostly in the 1930s and became adults in the 1950s—a decade or two before the baby boomers. The Silent Generation is sometimes so named because it was relatively overlooked, coming between "the greatest generation" and the raucous baby boomers. Many fought in the Korean War.

The "Silenteers" are now nearly the oldest residents in many neighborhoods. Many may soon downsize their homes or move to retirement communities.

Silicon Glen: Term for the tech sector of Scotland. It is applied to the so-called Central Belt triangle between Dundee, Inverclyde, and Edinburgh. This area also includes Glasgow.

Silicon Hills: Term used to describe the **Austin, Texas,** area beginning in the 1980s as many tech companies (including Dell) made homes there.

Silicon Prairie: Name for:

1. The **Dallas-Fort Worth, Texas,** area, due to its many tech and telecom companies.

2. The **Chicago-Naperville, Illinois,** area. (Other Midwestern areas also claim this title.)

Silicon Valley: Valley south of **San Francisco** that is home to an array of tech giants, including Apple, Google, and Facebook. Once a suburb of San Francisco, the area appears to have surpassed San Francisco in economic might. Centered around **San Jose. See also:** *superburb, Valley of the Kings.*

Single Awareness Day (SAD): Snarky alternative name for Valentine's Day.

Singlish: Variant of English spoken in **Singapore,** containing many Chinese, Malay, and "Indian" words.

sirenade: Term for the sound of a siren or a car alarm repeatedly going off late at night. Blend of the words "siren" and "serenade."

sirring: Unreasonably and annoyingly calling a slightly older man "sir." *Example: "Stop 'sirring' me! I'm only two years older than you!"* **See also:** *ma'aming.*

skate: 1. In workplace slang, to leave for the day before completing your duties. A term often used in restaurants. An example: when a waiter waits on his tables but leaves before cleaning his assigned dining area. **2.** To escape prosecution for a crime. *Example: Ten-year old son: "Dad, I heard that shady lawyer just had his sentence commuted. What does that mean?"*

*Dad: "Sounds like he **skated**, son."*

skater: A skateboarder or roller skater.

skater hater: Someone who *HATES* skateboarders.

skylight: A device to allow sunlight to enter a room, through the roof and ceiling. Viewed as Nature's "grow light" by those who grow herbal remedies.

sleep divorce: When a couple sleeps in separate rooms. Causes include snoring, differing schedules, or the desire to read or watch TV in bed.

"sleep-sleeping": Term which denote simply sleeping during an allotted sleep time, rather than sleepwalking, sleep-eating, etc.

Sloane Ranger: In the UK, a Sloane Ranger (or a Sloanie) was originally (in the 1980s) a young upper-class person, who has a fashionable lifestyle. The term is derived from **Sloane Square** in Chelsea, **London,** famed for its wealthy residents; and from the television character the *Lone Ranger*. Most aging Sloanies are now found driving **Chelsea Tractors** and many have relocated to the suburbs.

smarter than you look: Classic praise–insult combo, very common with teenage siblings. *Example:*

Twelve-year-old brother: "I got an A on my math(s) test today!"

Big sister: "Wow, you're smarter than you look!"

SMOG: 1. "Signal. Mirror. Over shoulder. Go!" A safe-driving slogan for beginners (or others) when changing lanes. Becomes unwelcome advice when backseat teens use this phrase on their parents. **2.** A blend of smoke and fog, a delight of Southern Californians, and others.

SNAFU: Situation Normal All "Fu**ed" Up. A military acronym for a challenging (to say the least) situation. *Example: "I tried to renew my car tags during lunch break. A total SNAFU."*

snarky: Sharply critical; snide. *Example: Handed a violation by her* ***HOA,*** *Phoebe became very snarky.*

soap dodger: An untidy or unkempt person.

so-called: Useful word that implies that something needs "air quotes" around it. Alternatively, the speaker can omit "so-called" and wiggle two fingers of each hand in the air to indicate the quotes. *Example: Have you tried her so-called soufflé?*

soccer: Familiar game in the burbs for kids and teens. The name began as a slang abbreviation of the term "association football" (asSOCia-tion). *Example: An old adage holds that soccer is a game of gentlemen, played by hooligans. Rugby is a game of hooligans, played by gentlemen.*

SoCo: Southern Comfort, a liqueur popular in the southern US. Its "secret recipe" reportedly contains whiskey, spices, vanilla, and sugar or honey. Basically, it contains everything you like (except perhaps coffee, and that is "fixable").

Sofa King low: Slogan for the Northampton, UK, based furniture seller Sofa King: needs to be said aloud to get the full effect. After several years of boasting their prices were "*Sofa King low*," censors forced the retailer to pull the ads in 2012.

soft opening: Marketing term noting when a restaurant will open with little advertising, later following with a well-publicized grand opening. As some comedians have noted, something about the name "soft opening" sounds questionable.

solar panel: Slang for a man's shiny bald spot on the top of the head. **See also:** *divot, hair helmet.*

Sopranos, The: Fascinating, lifelike TV show of the 1990s. The eponymous Sopranos family lived a typical life in upscale suburban New Jersey, ***except that*** dad Tony Soprano was a mafioso. It's not the first time mafiosos have been portrayed in the burbs. In the 1972 film *The Godfather,* main character Don Corleone moves his family to the suburbs in the 1940s. Ever wonder what a mafioso like Tony Soprano would do if his neighbor repeatedly parked in front of his (Tony's) house?

spam: Unwanted emails. The name comes from the Monty Python "Spam Song" in which a chorus of singers repeatedly interrupts the scene with a refrain of "Spam, spam, spam, spam."

Spam: A canned meat product marketed by Hormel. Said by some to be a word blend of "spiced" and "ham," although there are many explanations. One common explanation is "special Army meat." During the shortages of World War II, Spam was often viewed as a luxury around the world, and spam fritters are surprisingly popular to this day. An important element in Hawaiian cuisine.

Spam Museum: Museum chronicling the glories of Hormel's canned meat product in Austin, Minnesota. Notably the museum is in a converted big-box retail location, a former Kmart store. Too bad the museum isn't shaped like a can of Spam!

special: 1. Term sometimes used to denote education programs for those with learning disabilities or other special needs. **2.** Term used informally when someone has problems learning something. Can be used in either a friendly or unfriendly way.

spill the tea: To gossip, or to encourage someone to gossip.

splash: A "splash" or dash of liquor or soda in a cocktail, such as a splash of cola in Long Island iced tea.

spool: A mini swimming pool. A cross between a "spa" and a "pool."

Sprouts Farmers Market: Growing grocery chain with an emphasis on cheap yet healthful foods. Prevalent in the western and southeastern US. *Example: It has been noted that "Sprouts Farmers Market" is not a farmers' market, but a grocery store.*

square grouper: Slang for bales of pot found in the Gulf of Mexico when discarded from smugglers' boats or airplanes. Can also refer to the "haul" of fishermen who have become smugglers. *Example:*

South Floridian # 1: "Is your uncle still a fisherman?"

South Floridian # 2: "Yeah ... for square grouper."

squeak by: Usually-friendly term that means to barely pass an exam, or to barely be admitted to a program.

"Squeeze me.": Little children's version of "Excuse me!"

staircase wit: Slang term for thinking of the perfect witty answer or "comeback" just a moment too late. So called because you often think of the perfect answer while descending a staircase on the way home. Damn it! **See also:** *jerk storing, zinger.*

starter accountant: Someone's first accountant, who will generally be the cheapest one available. As a person builds wealth, he or she will seek out a more sophisticated accountant, often with greater knowledge of loopholes in the tax system.

starter divorce: The first, but perhaps not the last, divorce in someone's lifetime.

starter marriage: A person's first marriage. **See also:** *serial monogamist, starter divorce.*

starter retirement: Someone's first retirement from the working world. Can refer to aging rock stars who have a series of "farewell tours," or simply to the bloke down the street who overestimated his savings. Also a ha-ha name for a gap year. **See also:** *gap decade, gap year.*

STEM: Science, Technology, Engineering and Mathematics. A buzzword in many suburban school systems.

Stepford Wives: Satirical movie based on Ira Levin's 1972 novel, which poked fun at ultra conformity. The term "Stepford" or "Stepford Wives" has since become a half-joking label for cookie-cutter suburbs. Said to be loosely inspired by the real-life town of **Stamford, Connecticut.**

stoptional: Attitude of some drivers regarding stop signs, for whom stopping is "optional."

storm chasers: 1. Journalists, scientists, or amateurs who chase storms such as tornadoes for professional reasons or for thrills. **2.** Shyster contractors in the roofing trade (and in other professions) who show up in a town after a major storm. **See also:** *roof rats.*

struck oil at the altar: Texas slang for marrying into oil wealth.

strong as a mother: Term often seen on T-shirts and elsewhere, celebrating the toughness of many Moms.

student ghetto: Area traditionally found near universities, featuring low-rent apartments. Often a hodgepodge of old subdivided homes. Frequently home to bars, coffee shops, and once upon a time, record shops and bookstores. *Remember those?* In recent years, rents have climbed ever higher in these areas and many independent retailers have been replaced by chain stores. **See also: Jeremiah's Vanishing New York.**

study: A room devoted to reading or business activities and providing a refuge from family interruptions. To many dads, this was used as a sort of **man cave** before the term man cave existed. Reportedly a much sought-after feature in often rather compact Japanese homes.

"Stuff happens.": Expression used as an "explanation" for a sudden, unwelcome, change in behavior. *Example:*

Girlfriend: "What were you doing going around with that slut?"

Boyfriend: "Well, you know. Stuff happens."

stuffocation: Clutter. State of anxiety created by having too many possessions.

Sturdy Station: Brand of diaper-changing station found in public restrooms. Smart alecks sometimes cross out the first and last letters in "sturdy," resulting in "turd Station."

style-free zone: Snooty term for someone with little fashion sense. **See also: hobo-sexual.**

subbed: Subscribed, as in "subbed" to this or that YouTube channel.

submit: A troublesome word signifying submission. Just think about how often we are asked to promise to *Submit* before endorsing an electronic agreement.

suburbs: An area outside the city center mainly containing residences. Known to exist since at least Ancient Roman times. Mentioned by the Roman author Cicero, who referred to villas built on the outskirts of Rome as *suburbis*. (Cicero may have been happy to know that a suburb of Chicago is named for him.)

Suburban Outfitters: A recently coined nickname for clothing retailer Urban Outfitters. Based on the retailer's clientele, "Suburban Outfitters" seems more "fitting."

Suburgatory: Recent TV series with a new twist on the "city dwellers moving to the semi-whacked suburbs" theme.

sue: A verb, rather than a name, in many upscale suburbs. To remedy (or *attempt* to remedy) a situation with legal action. See also: *restraining order.*

suicide lanes: Reversible commuter lanes on automobile thoroughfares. So-called because unaware commuters can be trounced by oncoming traffic.

summer: For the well off, and to snowbirds, "summer" is a verb. *Example: "This year we're going to summer in Detroit."*

Sunnyslop: Not so friendly nickname for the north Phoenix, Arizona, neighborhood of Sunnyslope.

superburb: A suburb that has surpassed the core city of a metro area to become the largest city in terms of population. In some cases, the "superburb" also has greater economic clout. A term coined in *Suburban Dictionary. Examples:*

Oakland, California: superburb of San Francisco.

San Jose, California: superburb of San Francisco and hub of Silicon Valley.

suss: To figure out, to talk through.

SUV magnet: Condition of those driving small cars who inevitably find themselves parked between two oversized, poorly parked sport utility vehicles.

swearanade: Blend of "swear" and "serenade." The not-so-soothing sound created when the couple next door starts cursing at each other on their back patio. Generally grows worse as the weekend progresses and your neighbors become more intoxicated. At night-time, a "moonlight swearanade."

Swiss Army wife: A wife who is resourceful in all sorts of unexpected ways. Most excellent.

synthetic lawn: New and slightly more appealing term for artificial grass.

- T -

Table Mesa: Mesa on the northern outskirts of **Phoenix, Arizona.** Its name means "*Mesa Mesa,*" or "Table Table." Part of a long line of redundant place names, such as Picacho Peak (Peak Peak), also in Arizona.

talking story: Hawaiian term for storytelling or friendly idle conversation. An important part of life in **Hawaii.**

(a) talking-to: Understated suburbanese term for a "chewing out," or a scolding. *Example:*

Husband: "Well, last year I skipped my mother-in-law's birthday party."

*Wife: "Yeah, and you got a **talking-to!**"*

tattoo typo: Term for often-reported spelling errors in tattoos, such as "No regerts."

TBH: To be honest. Seen in texts and emails. Not necessarily a guarantee of honesty.

tearer-downer: A fixer-upper home that has fallen into such disrepair that more extreme action is required.

tenish: Term to describe a home selling for $10 million—give or take a million. Usually *does* feature a tennis court.

Tes-hole: A Tesla owner who is impressed with herself or himself and drives aggressively. Coined in *Suburban Dictionary.*

"text" book: Amusing book style in which the entire plot is told in text messages. An example is the 2019 book *TBH, Too Much Drama* by Lisa Greenwald.

"Thanks be to God.": The last line uttered by church goers in the Roman Catholic Mass. A saying of thanks for presenting Mass. However, schoolboys—probably for centuries—have jokingly considered it to mean: "Thank God that Mass is finally over!"

Example:

Parish priest: "Go forth, the Mass is ended."

*Schoolboy: "Thanks be to **God**!"*

"Thanks for sharing!": "Sarcastic response often heard after someone shares unwanted, overly graphic information.

"Thanks in advance": Rather common closing for an email in which the sender is saying, "I don't care what you think. Just do what I am saying. Thanks in advance." If your boss asks for help and writes "Thanks in advance," you might want to consider replying: "Forget it in advance."

"That escalated quickly": Remark heard when an exchange shifts rapidly from conversation to confrontation. Popularized by the movie, *Anchorman: The Legend of Ron Burgundy.*

"That is so Texas!": Slang expression, reportedly commonly used in Norway, that means something is "over the top"; crazy. This usage has been reported in *Texas Monthly* and on the website of BBC News.

"That makes one of us.": Useful retort in many situations, often conveying a lack of enthusiasm.

Example:

Twenty year-old, recently hired: "Wow, I love working here."

Forty-five-year-old co-worker: "Well, at least that makes one of us."

"That's a great question": A comment used in business meetings in which a question that was asked—perhaps by someone in cahoots with the moderator—seems to forward the moderator's agenda. Sort of a **"cherry on top"** in a boring meeting. Bad enough that the meeting is boring, but even worse: the meeting leader is pretending it's interesting or exciting.

See also: *shill.*

"That's your perception of it.": Icy suburbanese response to criticism.

throning: Spending time on the toilet, after one's business, to gain a few moments of quiet time. Sometimes used as a tactic to create a sort of temporary **man cave,** or **she-shed.**

thunder thighs: Large or heavy thighs. Often used jokingly or affectionately, but sometimes received less jokingly than it was intended.

Tidy Town: Charming Irish and Australian term for towns that have been lauded for being clean and litter-free. Some joke that an alternative competition could be launched, called "Least Tidy Town." In countries with a grimy image, a "Least Untidy Town" prize might be fitting.

" 'til you learn it": Useful addendum to a put-down.

Example:

Karaoke singer: "Mind if I sing that song again?"

Audience member: "Hey, no problem. Sing it 'til you learn it."

time suck: A person or activity that sucks your time. **See also:** *clock sucker.*

Example: "Visiting Costco on a Saturday afternoon is such a time suck."

tinsel-tooth: Time-honored kids' ribbing term for someone with braces.

TMI: Too much information. Often used when someone has revealed overly-personal or gross information.

too cool for school: 1. A student who thinks he or she is "too cool" for homework, gym class, or other tasks. **2.** Anyone who thinks normal guidelines do not apply in his or her case.

Too *school* for *cool:* Reverse label, usually friendly, for those who excel in school studies at the expense of a social life.

totes: Twee version of "totally", often seen in text messages. An example is "totes adorbs," meaning "totally adorable". Totes nauseating, to some.

toxic relationship: A relationship that is harmful for one or both parties.

trade-umvirate: A collective term for the three low-cost German-owned grocers rapidly growing in the US. **Aldi, Lidl,** and **Trader Joe's** form the triumvirate or "trade-umvirate."

trading paint: A low-key fender bender or automobile collision **See also:** *cute meet.*

treasure hunt: Term for a strategy used by retailers such as Costco or Trader Joe's who often wow shoppers with unexpected items.

tree nuts: Name given by some to eco-warriors who protest tree-cutting, by occupying trees in a developer's path. **See also:** *whale humper.*

tribal knowledge: An insider's knowledge in a particular area of expertise, often expressed in a "tribal language." Examples include unlisted menu items at some restaurants, available to insiders.

truck nuts, truck nutz: Truck or SUV "accessories" resembling human "balls" usually hanging from the rear bumper and visible to motorists. Police departments have had little success in banning these items, which thus far have been supported by free speech. Bicyclists have recently gotten in on this with taillights known as "bike balls." **See also:** *bike balls.*

trunk-or-treat: Growing trend of one-site trick-or-treating for kids on Halloween. Children and their parents gather at a church or similar venue. In the parking lot, hosts will offer candy from the trunk (or **frunk**) of their cars. The trunk becomes the "house" front door. A safer option than braving traffic with door-to-door trick-or-treating. **See also:** *frunk.*

trustafarian: A young adult (with wealthy parents) who takes on an aimless lifestyle, or a lifestyle that mimics that of low-income persons. A play on the word "Rastafarian."

two-backed beast: Vintage slang for a couple making love.

Two-Buck Chuck: Nickname for the popular Charles Shaw wine brand sold at Trader Joe's grocery chain. Formerly $1.99 per bottle, now at least $2.99 in most areas. Deemed acceptable in many "cases" by both wine snobs and cheapskates. That doesn't happen very often. **See also:** *trade-umvirate.*

two eyes open: Movie-goer slang for a movie which *at least* didn't put you to sleep. A play on "two thumbs up." **See also:** *damn with faint praise.*

- U -

U.C.L.A.: University of Caucasians Lost (among) Asians. Ha-ha name for the University of California, Los Angeles, which has attracted many Asian students for decades. **See also: *U.S.C.***

uglied out: An object, such as a car, that still functions but has become unsightly and unwanted.

"Umm...": Interjection that often means "I wasn't paying attention, so I need a moment to think of some sort of response."

understatement: A hallmark of suburbanese. Describing something as less of a problem than it really is. Understatement is sometimes used to be "nice"; but it's also often used to inject sarcasm.

Example:

Husband: "Our neighbor's yard could use a bit of work."

Wife: "That pigsty?! That's the understatement of the year!"

unvitation: A polite invitation, usually to a social function, that is not intended to be accepted.

Example: "We're having a cocktail party this weekend, but you'll probably be busy with the kids, won't you?"

update: To tell someone off; to give someone unwelcome news.

Example: "I just updated my neighbor about his shitty-looking lawn."

UPOD: Under-promise, over-deliver. A popular strategy in business and, for many, in life generally.

urban exploration: Sometimes called **urb-ex,** this pastime has a growing following. Exploration of locales such as defunct factories, sewers,
abandoned subway lines, foreclosed shopping malls, and other "overlooked" urban areas. In many cases, **urb-ex** involves trespassing. A
prized destination of urb-ex: abandoned amusement parks. **See also:**
(The) Labyrinth.

U.S.C.: 1. University of Spoiled Children. Nickname for the University of Southern California, which took on added sting after the recent
college admissions scandal. **2.** The University of South Carolina, called
variously "the first U.S.C.", "the other U.S.C.", or home of the Game-
cocks.

– V –

vacant neighbor: A nearby resident who is a bit of an airhead. *Example:* *"Walking down my street, first you pass the vacant lot, and then the vacant neighbor."*

Valley Girls, Valley Guys: Term popularized in the 1980s by rock legend Frank Zappa and his daughter concerning somewhat airheaded teenagers in the **San Fernando Valley** of metro Los Angeles. Zappa's daughter Moon Unit (her real name) was fourteen years old when they recorded *Valley Girl* in 1982. The term "Valley Guy" is also used for ditzy males in suburban Los Angeles.

Valley of the Kings: Nickname, popularized in *The Economist* magazine, for **Silicon Valley**. Centered around **San Jose, California** in the San Francisco Bay Area, it's considered the valley of CEOs and billionaires. Apple, Google, Facebook and other firms are based here. **See also:** *Superburb*.

Vampire facial: Gruesome cosmetic procedure in which your own blood is used to make your skin (supposedly) more appealing and more youthful.

victory lap: A circle or rotation that a golf ball makes on the lip of the hole before falling in.

vinairegrette: The feeling that you made a bad salad-dressing choice. A blend of "vinaigrette" (salad dressing) and "regret."

Vitamin N: Term for the healing power of Nature experiences. Refers to "therapeutic" acts such as Nature walks, camping, or simply listening to a bird song. **See also:** *May the forest be with you.*

Vitamin V: Viagra. A hardening substance.

Vlog: A video blog (web log), such as a motor-mouth friend or relative who frequently posts on YouTube, and expects you to stay up to date on their latest exploits at all times.

Volksmarch: In German, "people's march." Non-competitive group walking or hiking that began in Germany and has spread outward. ***Example:*** *I tried doing the Volksmarch, but my foot was sore and it ended up being more of a Volks-schlep.*

VSOP: Very superior old pale. Frequent note on brandy brands, especially those aged at least four years. (Or so the author has been told.)

- W -

walled garden: Shorthand term for the closed "ecosystem" of media and tech providers such as Apple, Inc.

wardrobe malfunction: Exposure of private parts, especially in public. Can refer to the act of exposing or to the excuse often given when this occurs: "a wardrobe malfunction."

Wasilla, Alaska: Suburb of Alaska's largest city, **Anchorage**. Famous (or to some, infamous) as the place where Sarah Palin entered politics. She was mayor of this city before becoming governor of Alaska. She later became the Republican candidate for vice president along with presidential candidate (and late Arizona senator) John McCain.

"Way to go, Einstein!": Vintage term used when a stupid blunder is witnessed. **Example:** *Don't you wonder if the expression was ever used on physicist Albert Einstein while he was alive, after he might have made an absentminded mistake? "Way to go, Einstein!"*

Wealth Belt: A term the *New York Times* uses to describe counties of north and central New Jersey that are home to an increasing number of millionaires. **See also:** *Whiskey Belt.*

wedgie: Time-honored teen prank in which someone's underwear is pulled upward from behind, leading to embarrassment for the recipient.

"Well, why didn't you?": Snide retort after someone talks about their intentions or goals. *Example:*

TV show director: "Well, what I wanted to do was to make a comedy that everyone could laugh at."

TV critic: "Well, why didn't you?"

wet leaves: English translation of Japanese term for husbands who are unemployed or retired. Sticking around home all day, the husbands are like "wet leaves" that wives cannot sweep away.

whacked: 1: Crazy, off-kilter. **2.** Done in or assassinated. A term associated with organized crime.

whale humper: A person overly-concerned about the environment. A notch or two above "tree hugger." **See also:** *tree nut.*

"What do you want?": Often heard response after someone gives an unsolicited compliment.

"When you say...": Intro to a sharply clarifying question that indicates that someone has been annoyingly unclear. *Example: "When you say, 'We need to clean up the house,' exactly whom are you talking about?"*

wheelie bin: Brit and Australian term for a wheeled garbage can or "bin." Usually called a dumpster in the U.S.

whip-round: British term for passing the hat for a joint cause, especially in an office setting. An example is pitching in for a birthday present. *Example: "Let's have a whip-round to buy Shirley a wedding present."*

Whiskey Belt: Famous upscale suburb north of **Copenhagen, Denmark.** The wealthy residents are said to drink whiskey, in contrast to the beer-drinking (loser) middle-class suburbanites.

white-bread: Caucasian in ethnic makeup or behavior. Can be a mild insult. A somewhat outdated term for the increasingly diverse burbs.

white rice: Caucasian folks who aspire to be, or act as if, they are Asian.

Wi-Fi wars: Term for arguments among neighbors who choose a name for their Wi-Fi networks that will anger (or amuse) their neighbors when broadcast in the vicinity. For instance, if you are sick of your neighbor's overgrown lawn, you could rename your Wi-Fi network "MowUFnLawn." Then you could check available Wi-Fi networks occasionally to see if your neighbor gets even by renaming his network.

wine o'clock: Happy hour. Vino drinking time, which varies from participant to participant.

wisenheimer: A smart aleck. Commonly found in homes with teens.

with-drawl: How a Southerner (in the U.S.) pulls out of an agreement.

Wookieepedia: An amusing online encyclopedia pertaining to all things *Star Wars* related. **See also:** *May the 4th.*

"Wow!": Expression which in suburbanese often means "I can't believe you *said that!*" Can also mean "You are really in deep shit right now." **Example:**

Husband: "Honey, you know that dress makes you look fat, don't you?"

Wife: "WOW!"

WTF: Exasperated plea for explanation, meaning "*What the f**k?*" Also expressed as "Whiskey, Tango, Foxtrot," the military phonetic rendition. *Example:*

Dad: "I can't believe you just texted WTF. You are not supposed to talk, or be texting, like that!"

Thirteen year old daughter: "Dad, that just means Wednesday, Thursday, Friday."

"Wull": "Well," but spoken in a way that indicates reluctance, or disagreement. *Example:*

Monica: "Thanks for picking up the tab, Ross."

Ross: "Wull, I thought we were going Dutch."

- X -

xeriscape: Gardening with little or no irrigation. From the Greek word for "dry," as in Xerox or xerography ("dry writing"). Popular in the western US, xeriscape has spread to other regions. The term is not "zero-scape" as some seem to think, although that "term" could work nearly as well.

- Y -

yacht rock: Light rock by (mostly) 70s artists including Christopher Cross, The Doobie Brothers, and Little River Band.

"Yeah, right!": Typical sarcastic response to a tall tale. Some say this expression is increasingly heard in the age of "fake news."

Example:

Frat boy # 1: "Yeah, well, my first time was with an Italian supermodel."

Frat boys # 2 through # 6, in unison: **"Yeah, right!"**

"Yes or no.": An exhortation for a quick decision.

Example: Mom: "Would you like lunch?"

Teenage son: "Well, what are my choices?"

Mom: "Here's your choices: **Yes, or no?!"**

YIMBY: Yes in my backyard. Pro-development movement that has sprung up in recent years, as a response to the **NIMBY (not in my backyard)** movement. YIMBies are active in cities where housing has become crazy expensive. YIMBies also often favor large-scale housing projects, to the disdain of single-family home proponents.

"You are entitled to your opinion." Icy way to make it clear you are disagreeing with someone.

"You got *that* right": Common suburbanese response (an interruption) when a person starts a complaint with a qualifier such as "I realize it's not your fault, but ..." *Example:*

Customer: "I realize it's not your fault, but..."

*Plumber: "You got **that** right!"*

"You must have smart parents.": Retort often heard from moms and dads when the kids start bragging.

"You poor son of a bitch": Expression saying "It sucks to be you."

Example:

Co-worker # 1: "My wife has been on a health kick lately, cooking all sorts of tofu-based dishes."

Co-worker # 2: "You poor son of a bitch."

"You taught me well.": Snarky response to all kinds of criticism in many households.

Example:

Big sister: "You sure are being a jerk tonight."

Little brother: "Yeah. You taught me well."

Young Adult, or **YA:** Category of books aimed at teenagers, optimistically called "Young Adult."

- Z -

za: Pizza.

Zenfandel: A state of Zen or bliss brought about by Zinfandel wine.

zinger: A put-down, insult, or comeback that "stings" the recipient. Often meant to be the last word in a conversation. **See also:** *jerk-storing* and *staircase wit.*

zitcom: A TV sitcom aimed at (often zit-faced) teenagers. The Disney Channel has a slew of such shows.

zombie foreclosure: Foreclosure in which a home is left vacant by a mortgage holder who thinks he or she must promptly leave their house after missing a payment or two. The borrower wrongly thinks that the lender is now responsible for the home. If the lender doesn't complete the foreclosure process, the home falls into legal limbo and into disrepair. Some homes remained in zombie status for years after the 2008 financial crisis.

Zonies: Nickname for Arizonans. Sometimes used snootily by Californians for Arizonans on vacation in "SoCal" (Southern California).

Example: "Can't go to the beach today. Zonies took up all the damn parking."

Author's closing note: If you enjoyed this book, please leave a review. Reviews help authors to provide you entertaining reads. Thank you!

Acknowledgments

To my wife, Thanh, who encouraged me while I wrote and researched. To my daughter, (my I.T. department), who helped with design and brainstorming immeasurably. Also, thanks for "updating" me when I misused teen slang. (At the moment, I'm picturing a 14-year-old rolling her eyes in disgust.)

To the folks in daily life—especially my co-workers—who have contributed many expressions and words.

I appreciate the gracious help I received from numerous authors and publishers while working on this book.

To editor Michelle Horn, who provided invaluable copy-editing. To bestselling author Ryan Quinn, who graciously did a proofread of this book and offered crucial suggestions. To editor Hugh Barker, who provided writing improvements and generously suggested amusing British expressions.

Thank you all!